RESTLESS

Finding Rest in a Restless World

You are an amazing young man!
Keep on for Jesus! He is SO
worth it!

Your friend.

333

TYLER A. ROBERTSON

Cover Design: Tyler Robertson
Editing & Formatting: Jamie Hicks and Kathryn Robertson

ISBN 978-1-66786-750-2
BookBaby
Pennsauken, NJ

Dedication

To the woman who holds my heart...

I love you, Kathryn Michele.

Table of Contents

Introduction

Papers flung everywhere: to-do lists, planners, business spreadsheets, three-ring binders, study notes, sermon notes, game and skit ideas for summer camp, and books that I'll never have the time to read...

"This is crazy!"

I check my phone for some temporary relief: Facebook. Twitter. Back to Facebook. No, I'm not old. I just hate TikTok (insert relevant eye-rolling emoji here).

I scroll YouTube for ideas for this or that. Remember I have to send a text to someone. Grab the fancy new book on my shelf. Put it back with yet another eye roll and big sigh. Finish sending my text. Stare off into space. Glance back at all the papers on my desk.

I beat my head against the wall. Well, I seriously contemplated it.

"Stop!"

I take a deep breath. Finally, about to break, I admit, "I can't do it. I just cannot do everything that *needs* to be done."

My stomach is aching, and my head feels like Venus and Serena Williams are playing tennis up there.

"Is this really what my life is going to look like?"

***

I grew up in a pretty average home. Nothing fancy. I was surrounded by the southern charm of just plain country folk and North Carolina humidity. I guess you can say I had it made in the shade—literally. That North Carolina humidity doesn't play around. Shade is a must in July.

I was an average boy. I played with toy guns, rode my bicycle with a baseball card between the spokes, and often visited Mamaw and Papaw's house.

My church and Christian school were the hub of everything I did. Youth activities, sports, school plays, student government, camp, choir—you name it, I did it. But I think one of the greatest blessings of my childhood was the person in charge of all I was involved with—my pastor. He was amazing in all respects! His faithfulness and compassion were unprecedented, and his daily walk mirrored Christ more than any man I've ever known. God only knows where I would be had it not been for my pastor's wisdom and guidance.

I think one of the greatest proofs of his sincerity and love for people came with the decision to start a summer camp. His heart was to reach young people for Christ, and he made every effort to do so. By divine orchestration, he started the church's camp in the hills of southern Virginia. You know, God's country.

That place would mean a lot to many people, especially this ole country boy. It was a place of solace from the crazy of everyday life. No school. No cell service. (Yes, we did survive.) No Internet. No TV. No distractions! Just God and His crisp, mountain breeze that swept the valley and refreshed every weary soul that passed by.

I was privileged to serve there for almost a decade. So many memories that I don't have time to tell: snakes in the dining hall, skunks in the cabins, tubing down the river, camper-counselor softball games. Yea, it was awesome! But out of all the summers of wild fun and spiritual revival, no summer would have as great an impact on me as the last summer that I served.

***

Back to my sad, depressive saga...

I was preparing for my last summer at my favorite place in all the world. Pulling my hair out was a daily ritual as I tried to get everything into place for several hundred screaming kids who would probably die of video game anorexia by the end of the week. And not only that, I had to make sure my business back home would survive the summer. Running a window cleaning company is not easy when you spend eight weeks of the summer in the middle of nowhere without cell service or internet.

As the days began to count down to the commencement of camp, my anxieties and fears began to surface. I knew those kids were worth every bit of effort and preparation; I just didn't know how I was going to do it all. Doubts filled my mind: and what once was a joyful song of a heart ready to serve God, was now a dreadful tune of frustration and restlessness.

Would I lose my business? Would my customers welcome me back after a whole summer away? Would I even make a difference in the lives of those kids?

I didn't have a clue.

Right before the launching of summer camp, God began to work.

I was out on the job and reasoning through a thousand possibilities. I was sick of the rat race in my head trying to figure it all out. I was about to break. Jerking the tools out of my truck and mumbling some sarcastic remarks, I put my headphones in to drown out the world around me.

I quickly surfed to one of my favorite preachers, Dr. Scott Pauley. His fiery spirit and humble attitude behind the pulpit don't compare to his genuine love for Christ. Growing up, I had heard his messages at youth conferences and had salivated over his ability to communicate God's truth. His messages just seemed to hit home with me. Maybe it was the Appalachian dialect or the Clark Kent hair, I don't know.

My thumb landed on a message entitled "Finding Rest in a Restless World."

"Yeah, I think I might need this one!" I chuckled as I pushed play.

That ordinary day on the job would be a monumental day for my journey. It was not so much a man's message or delivery, but the God of the message Who was present with me that day.

I rushed home to see the passage for myself.

"Come unto me, all ye that labour and are heavy laden, and I will give you rest. Take my yoke upon you, and learn of me; for I am meek and lowly in heart: and ye shall find rest unto your souls. For my yoke is easy, and my burden is light," (Matthew 11:28-30).

"Easy? Lord, this whole 6:00 a.m. to midnight camp schedule is not going to be easy! And I have a business to run!"

Slowly but surely, He began to show me my fast-paced life from His point of view. Sure, I was busy doing all good and moral things, but was my focus really on Him? Was my end goal a destination, or was it Jesus? Like an arrow swiftly finding its mark, Jesus began to pull back the ugly layers of my restlessness. He began to show me it was not so much a matter of the physical condition, but a colossal disruption of my soul that had left me in the grave of fear, discontentment, and unbelief.

Then it hit me.

I'm living like a lost man. I am living the life that Jesus saved me from—controlled by fear and not by faith. Look what Isaiah said about the wicked (lost) man:

"But the wicked are like the troubled sea, when it cannot rest, whose waters cast up mire and dirt. There is no peace, saith my God, to the wicked," (Isaiah 57:20-21).

This is the description of a restless soul—stuck in utter darkness and troubled day and night. This is more than a matter of stress or sleepless nights; it is an aching on the inside that screams when all is silent. It's the stirring in your heart that shakes with every worry. It's the pit in your stomach when fear's vice grip gets ahold of your thoughts. Restlessness is the monster that hides in the secrets of your past. Its father comes from our old Adamic nature and is passed down from generation to generation. It has destroyed many souls from the inside out and has carried away captives of God's precious children.

My friend, Jesus has not called his children to live a life of unrest! No! He has made a way for us to find rest in a restless world.

Restless: Finding Rest in a Restless World is two years' worth of prayerful meditation and a study of Christ through Matthew 11:28-30. It is a discovering and rediscovering of rest in a very restless world. This book is not a finding-yourself type quest for happiness. You will not have to dig that deep to understand it. So don't try to over complicate it. Soul rest is simple, as Christ intended it to be.

We will begin Part One with examining how we have gotten where we are. What is it about our world that is so restless? What are the direct reasons for a restless heart? What prescription has the world come up with to deal with the longing in their soul? You will come to find that the very things that the world proclaims as the cure to restlessness can in return only produce more restlessness.

In chapter 1, we will examine the Delusion of Prosperity. These are the lies that the culture has begged us to believe in order to find peace and happiness. Many of God's children have swallowed up these lies hook, line, and sinker:

· You will miss out.

- More stuff equals happiness.
- The more money you have the better of a person you are.
- Power only belongs to the rich.
- If you had more you could finally have rest.

This is the delusive ideology of the world that we must reject in order to follow Jesus' way of rest. We must stop pursuing **something** and start pursuing **Someone**. Our inward peace lies in the character of a Person, and that Person is worth pursuing.

The next reason for the restlessness within our souls is the Drive for Productivity, which we will discuss in chapter 2. Many people choose to medicate the hurt of their soul by simply getting busy. It's not just a matter of checking something off their to-do list, but it is an indictment on their character if they cannot be a success or build an exuberant empire. This is a persuasive violence as it will deceive you into thinking that you are making progress, when on God's time-table, you have stopped growing in His love and grace. You have worked hard to build your life and have forgotten God has made your hands for the work of His kingdom.

We will dive into several habits of toxic productivity:

- Work-a-holism
- Hyper Multitasking
- Neglect of the Essentials
- Hurry Sickness

These are habits that strip your mind from the gift of being present and stem from a heart desperate to stop. And before you know it, you are so busy that you begin to miss your life happening right in front of you. It's almost as if you have stepped into this virtual reality where interactions with people have become more like business transactions. But is this truly at the heart of our Lord? Was He so busy in His work that He could not stop to focus on another? Was He so self-absorbed in His own agenda that He could not help the hungry soul? I think you will find that our tendency is to be more like the restless man of Isaiah 57 than to be like Christ.

That moves us into the next reason of a restless soul: the Demand of Perfectionism. If having more or getting busy doesn't fix the pain of restlessness, then certainly being perfect will do it, right? Wrong! Perfectionism can transform a perfectly good character trait into a vice of selfishness and pride. It is why many people find it hard to lay their heads down at night because they can never meet up to the standards they have set for themselves. In chapter 3, we will put ourselves through the test of perfectionism and see if our rest got lost through the confines of our own making. We'll ask ourselves several questions:

- Are you extremely irritable?
- Would you rather just do things yourself so that they get done "right"?
- Do you have Eternal Syndrome where everything you do must have a strong sense of purpose, leaving no time for recreation?
- Do you procrastinate because it's just not good enough yet?
- Do you fear failure to the point that you never try anything that is hard?

We can often become enslaved to the high demands of perfectionism we place on ourselves. And that is where the restlessness creeps in. We aren't supposed to live by our own standards; we are supposed to submit in complete obedience to the standards that Christ alone gives.

The final reason in chapter 4 is the Dangers of Pleasure. Some medicate the restlessness in their soul by "getting after it." Sometimes they put unrealistic pressure on themselves, and see if they feel any different. But I believe one of the greatest narcotics of inner turmoil is the slow drift of a man into his comfort zone. We just want life to be easy. No problems. No heartaches. No cares. We have cultivated an environment inside the Christian church of isolation from the world. And I truly believe it's not for the sake of being separate from the world (as we'd like to think it is), but that we push the world away because we long to be safe and secure. We want relief from our wounds, but relief and rest are not the same thing.

So now in our new bubble of isolation we must shut out the noise from our own hearts. We reach for a socially acceptable narcotic to scratch the itch: drugs, alcohol, sex, overeating, binge-watching movies and shows, browsing social media for hours on end, pornography, etc. These are all pleasures that will only "do the trick" for a short time, but like a begging stray, it will eventually come loitering back for more.

These four reasons of restlessness are what we, in our best efforts, can come up with to find rest. They are produced from a restless heart in desperate need of God. But for every reason we are restless, Christ has a remedy! Part Two is all about how you can find rest in Jesus. Each chapter is Christ's direct rebuttal to our skewed view of peace and soul rest. Matthew 11:28-30 lays the foundation for your soul rest. Can you see it?

We believe the lies of the culture that prosperity is the key to our rest, but Jesus says, "*Come unto me.*" In chapter 5, we will learn how true rest is found in the person of Jesus Christ, and by learning Who He is, we can learn to have (and keep) rest. We will dive into His compassion, His consistency, and His closeness.

These are the characteristics of our Lord that breathe a cool sense of His love into our dry and desolate hearts.

We believe that productivity will merit the kind of rest we are looking for, but Jesus says, *"I will give you rest."* Soul rest is not something you can develop, strategize, or produce. It is given to you solely by the works of Jesus Christ. We will be reminded in chapter 6 that work is good, that God will not forget our physical needs, and that soul rest can be obtained through any circumstance. But one of the greatest lessons to be learned, is the power of nothing. Literally, the power behind putting Christ's desires above everything that what we feel or think is right.

We believe that setting our own standards for living will create the perfect environment for rest, but Jesus says, *"Take my yoke upon you, and learn of me."* In essence, Jesus is saying that in order to keep your mind and soul at rest, you must learn through a process. In chapter 7 we will enroll in the school of Christ and learn of His meekness and lowliness. We will dig deeper into the mine of Christ's humility and expose the filth of our own pride. It will not be a one-and-done decision, but it will take some time and patience to clean out our preconceived notions and embrace Christ's righteousness. There is no standard we can set, no environment we can create to ensure *"the peace of God which passeth all understanding."*

We believe that rest is simply a utopia of comfort and ease, but Jesus says, *"ye shall find rest unto your souls."* Why do we persist in searching for peace through worldly pleasures? It's because we do not believe His promise that if we *"come,"* we *"shall find rest."* In this closing chapter, we will deal directly with the problem of unbelief and why we run to the medication of the world to ease the pains of life. But if we truly believe in His promise, we will begin to see that He is enough.

So, if you are restless…aching to stop…longing to slow down…or finding your heart hurting when everything is quiet—this book is for you. Not because it will lead you to rest, but because it will lead you to Christ and His love.

It is in this love that we can find rest for our souls, for His love is the sweet melody that bows the strings to the revived life and gives man his song!

*Like the wave of the sea
That crashes day and night,
The soul of man can find no rest
For darkness is his plight.*

*But Christ does not leave him there;
In compassion comes his plea,
That all the weary shall find rest
"Come unto Me."*

PART ONE

The Reasons for Restlessness

CHAPTER ONE

The Delusion of Prosperity

H ave you ever been to New York City? If you have, you most likely know of a little suburb called Chinatown. Chinatown is a densely populated neighborhood that attracts many tourists with its Southeast Asian restaurants and shops. I remember my visit to Chinatown as a senior in high school; and I can assure you, it was an interesting experience.

I had heard word from others who had visited Chinatown that the venders were, shall I say, a bit on the "aggressive side." So, I thought I'd have a little fun and maybe come out with a bargain. I walked into a shop with a group of friends, and I heard a man say, "Psssst, come here!"

I saw no potential danger in a strange, dirty looking man ushering me into a small closet area behind the counter, so I hurried right over! Looking around in somewhat of a frantic pattern, he opened a drawer that was filled with all sorts of tiny items. He proceeded to tell me how very special I was being the only one in the store to see inside His "special" drawer.

He then told me something that I wasn't expecting.

He held up a "name-brand" wrist watch, and with a cheesy grin, proceeded to tell me that it was worth around $4,000! "But, my man, I will sell this watch to you, and only you, for the insanely low price of $20!"

My reaction shocked us both. I burst into laughter and said, "If what you're saying is true, then you are the worst salesman I have ever met!" I walked out of the store kind of feeling bad for being so harsh, but still chuckling on the inside.

You know our culture is much like that salesman. They try and try to sell us a cheap imitation of God's rest, and we often buy right into it. The truth is that someone has lied to us. Someone has looked us square in the eye and told us that money will fix everything. The business world has told us that our self-worth hinges on how much money we make. Hollywood has told us that wealth is the essence of power and prestige. And Wall Street has ignited a rage of addiction to the drug of the dollar.

One Wall Street banker said this about the desire for more: "We must shift America from a needs to a desires culture.... People must be trained to desire, to want new things, even before the old have been entirely consumed. We must shape a new mentality. Man's desires must overshadow his needs."

I would say to that Wall Street banker that his job has been successful. The culture has shifted. Most of us hardly realize what it means to actually need something in America. We are convinced by every fiber of our being that we need the newest iPhone, sportscar, designer clothes, or whatever. And then as we scurry to grab the greatest Black-Friday deal ever, we wonder, "Why am I doing this?" We breathe in the emotional high of a credit card swipe as we mutter to ourselves, "I don't really need this!"

The accumulation of stuff is a cultural phenomenon that has polluted our minds into thinking "the more the merrier" even if we don't have room for it. Storage units in America are a $38 billion industry with 2.3 billion square feet of storage space. Someone figured up that if we gave every American seven feet of storage unit space, we could literally house everyone in the United States. And if that's not enough, we build buildings behind our homes, make space in our attic, fill our garage with everything but the car and lock it all away behind a privacy fence, just to one day give it to our children to eventually sell in a yard sale.[1]

We are convinced that the Land of ER really does exist; therefore, we will do everything in our power to get there. Oh! You haven't heard of it? This is land that has no geographical location. No topography or beautiful landscape. In fact, no one has ever been there before. Many wish to live there, maybe even just visit for a short time; but for some strange reason, there's not a clear path that leads to this destination. Have you figured it out yet? It is where people wish to be smartER, bettER, fastER, strongER, richER...you get the point.

It's a place that people strive for, but never hit the mark. It's the bloody battlefield up the steps of a corporate ladder or political position. It's a place that once "reached," people look back and feel like it's not at all what they wanted. This fire on the inside is fueled by a "more is better" mentality that has led men into a drunken stupor of "hoardom."

The truth is, we have let our restless hearts lead us on a chase for the world's riches, and all the while Jesus is pleading: *"No man can serve two masters: for either he will hate the one, and love the other; or else he will hold to the one, and despise the other. Ye cannot serve God and mammon [the things of the world,]*" (Matthew 6:24). This is the epitome of living a double life. We want wealth, health, and happiness; and we want it so badly that we will sacrifice our relationship with Jesus to get it.

My youth pastor used to often say, "If you sell out God for minimum wage now, you'll sell Him out for a lot less later on in life." I can testify that there are many young people that I grew up with that did not heed to his warning and gave their part-time job the first place in their lives. They boasted of their part-time wages, but unfortunately had the part-time mentality about Jesus too. I would meet them sometime after we were out of the youth group, and their countenance would scream that they weren't happy. Sure, they had the job they wanted and got to finally be out from under the thumb of the church, but it was obvious the world didn't deliver for them like they had hoped.

"A double-minded man is unstable in all his ways," (James 1:8).

The love of prosperity is a blazing neon sign of a restless soul. *"For the love of money is the root of all evil: which while some coveted after, they have erred from the faith, and pierced themselves through with many sorrows,"* (I Timothy 6:10). In my opinion, one of the greatest deterrents of someone trying to wholeheartedly follow Jesus is the relentless pursuit of the land of ER.

Now let me clear the air a little. This doesn't mean that a Christian cannot be well off or have nice things. There is a skewed view in some Christian circles that you must either be poor and godly, or rich and worldly. I think there is a mistake on both sides. Just read some of the great Christian biographies—William

Borden, D.L. Moody, Charles Spurgeon, etc.—and you'll find that God allowed much wealth to pass through their fingers. The only difference was that their wealth did not have them, Jesus did.

When we have substituted the sufficiency of Jesus for the flashy new thing on the shelf, we have believed the lies of the culture and have fallen head-long into a cycle of restlessness.

Let's look at some of the lies of our culture and debunk them with the truth of God's Word.

You Will Miss Out

The feeling of missing out is gut-wrenching for most people.

· Friends are at a party, but you have to work.
· Family is on a cruise, but you are sick at home.
· Someone, somewhere, is having it better than you!

Feel like a loser yet? This desire of going without is a monetized scheme of the business world. If they can get you to think you are missing out on something that everyone else has or is doing. Then they can get you to buy a book, two books, three books or whatever product they are selling. Just look at the titles in the financial categories on Kindle:

· *The Secret Habits of a Millionaire*
· *The Mystery Behind Building Wealth*
· *The Hidden Steps to Early Retirement*

If someone can make you feel like you're not socially acceptable until you are "in the know," then he holds you and your wallet captive.

But what exactly are you really missing out on? I'll tell you: the pain of sin, guilt from regrets, a divided family, unmet desires, shallow relationships. Do I need to go any further?

Oh yes, my friend! When you choose to follow Jesus, you miss out on a lot of things, but I promise, what you gain is beyond what you can comprehend.

Paul said it this way, *"But what things were gain to me, those I counted loss for Christ. Yea doubtless, and I count all things but loss for the excellency of the knowledge of Christ Jesus my Lord: for whom I have suffered the loss of all things, and do count them but dung, that I may win Christ,"* (Philippians 3:7-8).

I think it's important to note that Paul still suffered as a follower of Jesus. What was the difference? Jesus. He literally gained all of Christ and that was enough for him. And he wasn't always a poor beggar. Prior to salvation, Paul had wealth, a high position in the Sanhedrin, and plenty of prestige—he was loaded. But when Christ came onto the scene of his life, all those things looked strangely dim in the light of His glory and grace.

The problem we have with Paul's perspective is that most of us are not willing to lose what we have to gain Christ. Why? Because, simply put, we believe Christ is not enough. The fear of missing out on what the world promises is much too hard of a pill to swallow.

It was the same for the prodigal. Do you remember? He left all and fled to a far country and *"there wasted his substance on riotous living,"* (Luke 15:13). I believe the young man had his eyes set on the far country long before he ever left the father. I wonder what he missed at the father's house while restlessly scrounging up the slop from the pig pin? I wonder what we have missed out on with our Father because we believed the lie of the far country that "the grass is always greener on the other side." Are we really missing out?

More Stuff Equals More Happiness

"Everyone is on a happiness quest," my Sunday school teacher used to say. And how right he was. Everyone is looking to be happy, to feel the chills of a wholesome life, where problems are far away. But what if we are convinced our happiness comes with a price tag? What if we think in order to be happy, we must have a certain amount of money coming in each paycheck or have a lot of real estate in our name?

According to the Nature of Human Behavior, once we reached a certain household income—$105,000 in the United States, $95,000 globally—more income "tended to be associated with reduced life satisfaction and a lower level of well-being." [2]

More money is more likely to compensate with anxiety, depression, and substance abuse than it is to give you a long-lasting smile.

I am reminded of a story that my mentor told often. It was about a young man who had surrendered his life to preach. He was a good-looking boy with a lot of promise waiting for him. After he graduated high school, he got his eyes set on the "far country." He became discontent with the path God had chosen for him. Entangled in his own plans, he dropped out of Bible college and married his girlfriend back home. He went on to be a very successful business man and was able to provide substantially for his family. But if you were to talk to him today, he would tell you, "I have everything I want—cars, nice house, etc.—but I know I'm out of the will of God."

For a Christian, joy cannot be found outside the boundaries God has established. It is only through the parameters of His will and Word that we can satisfy our hearts and truly be happy.

"Happy is he that hath the God of Jacob for his help, whose hope is in the LORD his God," (Psalms 146:5).

The More Money You Have, the Better Person You Are

Have you seen the lottery sign lately? I can guarantee you that no matter how much money the Power Ball is right now, it is more money than I will see in my lifetime! What crosses your mind when you see those numbers? You're probably like everyone else that thinks of all they can accomplish with their millions. We say silly things like, "I'd give it all away!" or "God, if you'd just give me a chance, I'll do a lot of good with it!"

We cannot falsely conclude that our abundance will magically change us into the people we wish to be. More money will not change our selfish natures into selfless ones. Take it from the capuchin monkeys. Seriously.

According to a study from Yale's Comparative Cognition Lab, monkeys are not as selfless as you may think. "In an experiment aimed at figuring out monkeys' willingness to share, researchers placed computer screens in front of their capuchin monkey study participants and had them complete a touchscreen task that led to food being delivered to other monkeys. Surprisingly, results showed that the capuchin monkeys, thought to be prosocial and cooperative from previous research, did not end up delivering food to a partner. The study was published in the journal Behavioral Sciences." [3]

There is a part of a monkey's nature that drives it to look out for its personal needs. It's a survival mentality that keeps their eyes keen to areas of opportunities where a physical need can be met. When additional opportunities arose, its inclination is to hoard and not to share.

Just because you have a lot of nice things doesn't mean you will automatically be inclined to have the heart of a giver. In fact, the opposite is often found to be true. That is because money is not the standard by which we measure our integrity. Some people think that the status of their material wealth is a result of the quantity of their faith. If they don't have faith, they will be poor. If they have enough faith, they will be rich. I strongly believe this is anti-biblical. Let me explain.

Poverty is not always a result of personal sin. I think we all know and understand that sin brings suffering and pain. But consider our fearless friend Job. Ah yes! The man who had everything stripped from his hands only to be left with a wife that wanted him to curse God and die. Then his friends thought his trial was a direct result of his disobedience to God. But actually, God made it clear that Job's trials were not a result of sin or disobedience, as He declared often that Job's character was *"perfect and upright."* Job 1:22 goes on to say, *"In all this Job sinned not, nor charged God foolishly."*

Suffering is actually promised for the one who takes up his cross and follows Jesus. If all suffering was a result of personal sin, then what about the missionaries who choose to labor in third world countries without easy access to basic essentials? Are they not exercising enough faith? I would say on the contrary. Also, look at the life of Jesus. He chose to be homeless. He was born in a manger. He was a carpenter by trade. But did Jesus lack faith in God? Of course not. He chose to live in complete obedience to God no matter the material outcome. Now let's flip the coin.

Prosperity is not always a result of personal obedience. It is a pure fact of biblical literacy that when we are obedient to God, God will bless us. But does this mean that God will make us rich if we keep the "Big Ten"?

"I am the true vine, and my Father is the husbandman. Every branch in me that beareth not fruit he taketh away: and every branch that beareth fruit, he purgeth it, that it may bring forth more fruit. Now ye are clean through the word which I have spoken unto you. Abide in me, and I in you. As the branch cannot bear fruit of itself, except it abide in the vine; no more can ye, except ye abide in me. I am the vine, ye are the branches: He that abideth in me, and I in him, the same bringeth forth much fruit: for without me ye can do nothing," (John 15:1-5).

By abiding in Christ, we in essence are tapping into all that He is and the blessings that He brings. But the real question is what kind of blessings? John 15:16 tells us, *"Ye have not chosen me, but I have chosen you, and ordained you, that ye should go and bring forth fruit, and that your fruit should remain."*

The blessings that God gives are eternal. They are fruit that remain forever. This doesn't mean He never blesses us with material things here on earth, it just simply means that whenever we are obedient to God, we cannot expect wealth and health by the world's standards. But we can rest assured that if we steward what God has given us (no matter the quantity), we will obtain treasures in heaven *"where neither moth or dust doth corrupt and thieves do not break through nor steal,"* (Matthew 6:20). Our lasting rewards are something the world cannot give or take away.

So, what's my point? Material riches do not always reflect the heart of the individual. If poverty is not always a result of personal sin, and prosperity is not always a result of obedience, then it's safe to conclude our financial status is not a pure reflection of who we are. Our goods never merit our godliness and our godliness will not always merit more goods.

Well, what about the Matthew 6:21? *"For where your treasure is, there will your heart be also."* Read it again carefully. It says nothing about the quantity of your treasure, but where you choose to put it. That is where you will find your heart. When you are a good steward of the blessings that God gives you, and your belongings have their proper place in your life, it is then that you will receive the blessings of a Christ-like heart and reap the fruits of the Spirit: *"love, joy, peace,"* (Galatians 5:22). Did you see that? Peace.

Power Only Belongs to the Rich

Some people are not as much enamored with wealth as the power that it claims to give. People want an elevated platform with a bird's eye view of their kingdom. It is a scratching to the itch of being "on top of the world," above the rest of the competition. Listen to what Sam Polk, a former Wall Street broker, said about his past profession:

"We're smarter and work harder than everyone else, so we deserve all this money—for what it is: the rationalization of addicts. From a distance I can see what I couldn't see then—that Wall Street is a toxic culture that encourages the grandiosity of people who are desperately trying to feel powerful." [4]

Our world is full of people who seek the power to control their lives. "If I were rich, I could go anywhere, see anything! I could live the life I've always wanted!"

If that is your way of thinking, you're absolutely right. You could do a lot more: buy VIP tickets to the Super Bowl, buy the lake house you've always wanted, finally quit on your crummy boss that overworks and underpays you.

You would have control of your life. But here is the question. Should you have control of your life?

The reality is that many Christians believe the lies of culture because they want to call the shots. Just because you have the power to make a decision, doesn't mean you should. The moment you invited Jesus into your life, a war of the wills commenced. This is the battle of your flesh and God's Holy Spirit. Only One may sit on the throne of your life. Whomever you allow to take the seat will be the one to whom you give the power to control every facet of your existence. But with power comes great responsibility. So, who is more responsible? You or the Holy Spirit? Well, let's compare resumes.

Your heart is desperately wicked. You cannot trust your emotions. You do not have much power over your circumstances. You cannot change time and its effect on you. You cannot promise tomorrow. Your pride is all you have to live by without Jesus. Selflessness is often hard to come by. You cannot love unconditionally. Your mind and body become weak and tired. *Restless* is the best word that describes you when you don't start your day with Jesus. You are not perfect (more on this later).

The Holy Spirit's heart is pure. His instructions and wisdom can always be trusted. He has the power to change your life and circumstances. He is already in your tomorrow. He will not force His will on you. Selflessness is one of His most beautiful qualities. He is the great healer and redeemer of the soul. His love knows no bounds. In fact, He *is* love. He never sleeps or becomes tired. He is the originator and the giver of soul rest. He is indeed perfect in every way!

So, who are you going to trust to call the shots? It's true, wealth will give you some control of your life, some power. But powerful kings have fallen because of deceiving counsel. You cannot expect the world to look you in the eye and tell you the truth. You cannot expect to look deep within your deceptive heart and find peace and rest. Just because it feels right in the moment, doesn't mean that it is right for the future. And come on! Who likes to be lied to? I don't know about you, but I hate to be deceived or lied to. I feel cheated and abused. I feel worthless on the inside and foolish for ever trusting anyone again.

The world wants you to believe that power and control only belong to those who are wealthy. But the truth of the matter is, that some of the most powerless people in the world live in an abundance of riches. They have a lot of nice stuff, but only an empty heart to show for it. They spend the rest of their lives finding no real meaning and satisfaction. Why? Because they have believed the lie that rest will come in the security of their riches.

What lies of the world have you believed in regards to prosperity? What vain pursuit has become the anthem of your life?

If prosperity is not the answer for restlessness, then what is?

Oh I know, let's get busy!

CHAPTER TWO

The Drive for Productivity

Have you ever been asked, "How are you?" and heard yourself repeating the answer: "Good, just busy." I have too. Busyness has become a staple of honor in our culture. We live in a society that praises the exhaustion of the business man or woman. It's the status quo to have a full schedule as well as productive "leisure" time.

Thomas Merton once called "the rush and pressure of modern life [a] pervasive form of contemporary violence."

Did you catch that? *Persuasive violence.* I don't think there is a better way to describe our accomplishment-driven society. Toxic productivity has destroyed much of the institution of the home and has sent men spiraling into a snare of regretful priorities. But "getting after it" is the socially acceptable thing to do. We allow our relationships to crumble to mediocrity just as long we get the promotion or check off our vitally important lists of to-dos.

Unfortunately, this way of thinking has seeped into the Christian community and is masked as passion.

"Oh, that person has such passion for what he does!" we hear people say.

There is a vast difference between passion and devotion. I believe passion is God-given; but just like everything else, it must be placed into the correct parameters of His will and Word. Much of Christendom, I'm afraid, has fleeted off on an affair with the twin gods of accomplishment and accumulation.

Hosea gives an explicit cry for mercy for the children of Israel regarding their worship of obtainment and productivity. Listen to his revelation of Israel's heart in chapter 14: *"Take your words, and turn to the LORD: say unto him, Take away all iniquity, and receive us graciously: so we will render the calves of our lips. Asshur shall not save us; we will not ride upon horses: neither will we say anymore to the work of our hands, ye are our gods: for in thee the fatherless find mercy."*

Is it possible for a child of God to worship a man-made idol, to worship the labor of his hands? Absolutely. An idol is anything that takes the place that only Christ is worthy of. Anything. That means something bad or something good.

We, like the children of Israel, can take the God-given desire for work and use our hands for our own purposes instead of God's. The drive to accomplish can be distorted into a means of self-exaltation and self-sufficiency. We love what we do because we are the ones making our own way or setting the trend. We literally begin to worship our work because it is our own creation, and no one else can take credit for it. See the idol part of it yet?

What we choose to put our hands to is ultimately where our hearts are. We see this in the beginning of Scripture. A world that was desperately out of tune with its Creator began to busy itself with empty projects, thus building on unsure foundations. And remember what happened to the foolish man who built his house upon the sand? Splash! Yea, not good.

What Are You Building?

In Genesis 11, we find a people laying out the plans for a rather noteworthy project.

"And they said, Go to, let us build us a city and a tower, whose top may reach unto heaven; and let us make us a name, lest we be scattered abroad upon the face of the whole earth," (vs. 4).

Man sought to build something of earthly significance and value—a name for himself. The Tower of Babel reached higher and higher with every feeble effort to become great, and it displayed the desperation of man's heart without God.

We live in a world of builders. Men vigorously indulge themselves in their lives, wishing to build their own fleshly kingdom. They nurture and dress their "castle" with sparkly things and show off their bounty to their friends. Their toys only become bigger, and their youthful desires are just repackaged into adult experiences. They grow older, but often they do not mature.

There was one man in the midst of life-builders that saw a more precious blueprint of heavenly design. Abraham. Maybe you've heard of him. He was the guy you sang about as a kid in everyone's favorite song: "Father Abraham." If I just got that dreadful song stuck in your head—you're welcome.

Abraham was a man not concerned with building his life, but rather with building an altar.

"And the Lord appeared unto Abram, and said, Unto thy seed will I give this land: and there builded he an altar unto the Lord, who appeared unto him. And he removed from thence unto a mountain on the east of Bethel, and pitched his tent, having Bethel on the west, and Hai on the east: and there he builded an altar unto the Lord, and called upon the name of the Lord," (Genesis 12:7-8).

Abraham journeyed to a land that he did not know because he was more concerned with His God than with his comfort. He understood the importance of building an altar wherever God planted him; and if he gave God his hands, then God would give the increase.

There is a wonderful lesson for all of us here. We are pilgrims. Tent people. Strangers in a far country. So why do we waste countless amounts of energy on building our castles of comfort? We busy ourselves with temporal things, while Christ is left outside of the door gently knocking.

And isn't it crazy the ways we gripe about how busy we are, and yet we are not willing to give up something on our forty-five pages of urgent to-dos. And we always think we will get to what is truly important after we get things done.

If I can just get to this weekend, then I'll be fine.

If I can just push through this time, then we can get to family vacation.

Some of the best doctrine I've heard on this philosophy comes from a pretty spectacular children's story: *Winnie the Pooh.* I believe the story of Christopher Robin has some life lessons we can all take away.

I remember one instance in particular when Christopher Robin is all grown up. He has a beautiful wife, little girl, and a good paying job.

His work is rather pressing on him, and his stuffy-nosed boss asks him to work the weekend. Problem. Christopher had already promised his little girl that they would spend the weekend at his childhood summer home. But Christopher Robin sides with his boss and breaks the news to his wife over dinner (to which he was late). The pressure begins to build in Mrs. Robin's face.

You can imagine the thoughts that scurried through her mind as she earnestly tried to keep it together. But this was not the first time she had been disappointed by her husband. In fact, this was the last straw.

Rising from her seat, she cuts an evil eye to her husband. Slowly she points her finger at him. Then she says something that I honestly hope I never forget.

Christopher quickly tries to console her: "If I can just work hard now, then..."

"Then what?" Mrs. Robin interrupts. "Christopher, your life is happening now. It's right in front of you."

That hit me. "Your life is happening now." So often I get infatuated with the future that I fail to joyously experience the present. It's like my senses are numb to my current circumstances because my mind is always in tomorrow. And even when the things I obsessively plan for arrive, I can't stop and enjoy them.

Trying to do can literally enslave you if you let it. Let's go back to the children of Israel. Do you remember what their lives were like before God delivered them from Egypt? It was constant work. Nonstop, nose-to-the-grind (literally), beat-you-into-a-pulp type of labor. They were enslaved to the god of Pharaoh and isolated to a life of misery.

There's a big bully on the street in modern American culture who, like Pharaoh, is enlisting God's people for the devil's purpose. And he confines the saints; not usually with gross sins such as murder, immorality, or drug abuse, but with simply putting them to work. And at the end of the day, this bully sits on the stock pile of his riches while God's people have nothing left to give to Jesus.

Perhaps you've heard the cliché, "If the devil can't make you sin, he'll make you busy." There's a lot of truth in that. But let's break it down. No, not in a juke and jive kind of way. Trust me, nobody wants to see that. Let's get specific to what it is that we run to instead of Jesus; what habits are formed by the enslavement of a restless—I mean—busy soul?

Work-a-holism

This is borderline laughable. It's hard for our brains to compute something as good as work being an intoxicating substance that strips the mind of awareness and the senses from emotion. But it's not a joke. Work-a-holism is a real substance abuse problem that strips us from the gift of being present. My youth pastor and now father-in-law used to say: "Be where your feet are!" Why? Because sometimes we can get so tangled up with an end goal that we fail to stop and recognize the beauty of the moment.

It's like when the little nag in your head won't let you leave your work problems at work, but instead tells you to bring them home with you. You just can't stop thinking about what is left to do.

Frantically, you search for a narcotic to scratch the itch and end up cleaning out your closet for the hundredth time or dusting off the chandelier hanging from your cathedral ceiling.

By the time you have medicated some of the problem, you realize the kids are in bed with a mumble of goodnight and there's a cold supper you haven't eaten yet. Or if they are still awake, you have nothing left of yourself to give them. Your soul is spent and your mind still racing. That is why they call this type of person a work-a-holic; because, like alcohol, work can strip time from your hands and decimate the relationships that matter the most.

Hyper Multitasking

There is a reason this cliché exists: "Jack of all trades, master of none." Okay, so I don't know who Jack is, but we should definitely be friends because we have way too much in common. I live in a delusion that I can literally be the best at everything I put my hands to. I can't just be a golfer; I've got to beat everyone I play. I can't just play the guitar; I've got to make the strings dance like Andres Sergovia. I can't just write a blog post; it's got to be a book. I just want to do it all.

We get ourselves into a lot of trouble when we try to do everything all at once. We think we have to experience everything. Go here, do that, see this. We paralyze ourselves by trying to have a widespread menu, while our quality of life is pretty sub-par.

Think about the picturesque teen today. He is sitting in a Lazy Boy, with headphones in and listening to music, playing Xbox with his friends, watching the game on another TV, texting a buddy about the new *Star Wars* movie coming out, and trying to somewhat psych himself up to do his math homework. Yea, I'm sweating just typing all that out. While we laugh at how ridiculous that sounds, we often do the same thing, just in an adult, sophisticated kind of way. We medicate our restlessness by trying to drown it out with the world's alluring fancies.

But why play such a dangerous game with your life? There are actually alarming consequences of multitasking.

Guy Winch, a licensed psychologist and author of *Emotional First Aid: Healing Rejection, Guilt, Failure, and Other Everyday Hurts*, gives these conclusions about multitasking:

· It can cause memory loss.
· It increases distract-ability. (Plainly said, you can walk into traffic and—well—die! All from trying to cross the street and choose which episode of "The Dave Ramsey" podcast you want to listen to.)
· It can give you an addiction to the universe inside your pocket—aka your phone.
· It is proven to increase chronic stress.
· It increases depression and anxiety.

Acting like you have super powers can leave you a super mess. You are intrinsically and uniquely human. Stop trying to be someone else's super hero. I promise it's not all up to you.

Neglect of the Essentials

There is a desire in all of us to get something done, but sometimes it comes with a price. We stay up late at night finishing that twenty-page research paper that we procrastinated on. We get such a rush of busyness that we fail to eat lunch. Friends, that's not healthy.

This is neglectful to the basic essentials our body needs in order to function as God intended. We are triune beings made in the image of God with a responsibility to nurture our mind, body, and soul. To be basic, we at least need the following essentials:

· Eight hours of sleep a night
· Daily exercise
· Nutritious diet

Not taking the time for the essentials results in constant fatigue, weight gain, and frequent sicknesses per year. Our rush of being productive is fueled by the caffeinated beverage of choice that stimulates momentarily and comes crashing in as a serious meltdown. We are restless at night and can't go back to sleep no matter how hard we try.

Listen closely. What is your body telling you? Maybe enough is enough.

Hurry Sickness

Yea, it's a real thing. John Ortberg put it this way: "Hurry is not just a disordered schedule. Hurry is a disordered heart." [5]

Did you just feel a laser beam come between your eyes? I did. Sometimes I get in such a hurry. It drives me crazy and my wife too. It's like I have all this pent-up energy to be somewhere all the time even if it's a weekend and there's nowhere to be.

Ever been there? It's just a feeling of getting past what is in front of you so you can get to the next thing, and the next thing, and the next thing. You literally "next thing" yourself to the grave.

My father-in-law used to drive me crazy on the golf course. Partially because he was my golf coach in high school, and so I always felt his analytical glare as I stood over the ball, but mainly

23

because we just play the game vastly differently. I am the type of golfer that takes my time, slows it down and breathes in the intoxication of fresh cut Bermuda grass on a cool spring evening. I get my money's worth out of the experience on the course. It soothes me and repels my mind from the pressures of life back at the office.

My father-in-law did not always play the game like me. He was on the other end of the axis in the golf world. It was one practice stroke, step to the ball and hit it. If the shot was good, he'd strut back to the cart with the "I totally meant to do that" look on his face; but if the shot was sub-par, he'd always say, "Well, I'll get better." There was always a mentality of rushing the shot so you can get to the next one and go to house. As for me, no way! I'm taking my time!

To his credit, he has recently learned to slow down and enjoy the journey of eighteen holes, and it pains me to say that I really enjoy playing with him now.

If we are not careful, we will deceive ourselves into thinking life is all about the product, instead of actually enjoying the process.

"For many of us the great danger is not that we will renounce our faith. It is that we will become so distracted and rushed and preoccupied that we will settle for a mediocre version of it. We will just skim our lives instead of actually living them." [6]

Rosemary Sword and Philip Zimbardo, authors of *The Time Cure*, give us these as symptoms of hurry sickness:

- Moving from one check-out line to another because it looks shorter/faster

- Counting the cars in front of you and either getting in the lane that has the least or is going the fastest
- Multitasking to the point of forgetting one of the tasks [7]

I don't know about you, but I don't want to just "skim" through my life. I don't want to get to the end, look back and think that I missed out on life's amazing moments simply because I was in such a hurry.

Michael Zigarelli from the Charleston Southern University School of Business conducted the Obstacles to Growth Survey of over twenty thousand Christians worldwide. Here is his hypothesis:

"It may be the case that (1) Christians are assimilating to a culture of busyness, hurry and overload, which leads to (2) God becoming more marginalized in Christians' lives, which leads to (3) a deteriorating relationship with God, which leads to (4) Christians becoming even more vulnerable to adopting secular assumptions about how to live, which leads to (5) more conformity to a culture of busyness, hurry and overload. And then the cycle begins again." [8]

See the digression? Productivity cannot give us the rest for our souls. It may make us more tired, resulting in a slightly deeper sleep, but the drive to be productive is just a mask to cover the secrets of a restless heart.

***

So if productivity is not the answer, then what is?

CHAPTER THREE

The Demand of Perfectionism

I remember as a kid doing some, shall I say, funny things. I mean come on, I was the only boy among five sisters; a man's gotta do what a man's gotta do to keep himself entertained. I remember one gloriously idiotic day in particular. I call it The Commencement of My Inner Evil Knievel.

My stepdad was rebuilding a deck onto the side of our house. Side note, the old deck came crashing down on top of my new Roadster bicycle and literally snapped it in half. I shall never forget that day. Hats off. A moment of silence for Roadster please.

Anyway, this deck was coming along nicely, and it would soon be a great place for grilling and relaxing on a cool night. I scurried outside to see what progress had been made, and I was surprised to see no railing on the deck. Of course, he had not quite finished the project, but I figured I'd try out the new deck anyway. Don't jump to a conclusion. It's not what you think.

I tiptoed my way up the stairs and onto the elevated platform. The north end of the deck was only about three feet tall; but since our house was built on a hill, the backend was much higher. Peering my head over the edge, I looked down to about an eight-foot drop. And then my genius struck me! Well, sort of.

I rushed inside and grabbed a beach towel out of the bathroom cabinet. Today was my day. I was going to be—drumroll please—a paratrooper. Yes, the guy that jumps out of airplanes and whistles back down to earth at exuberant speeds. It could have possibly been a slight inspiration from Mary Poppins, but I'll stick with the manlier narrative.

I was ready. Towel—I mean, parachute—in hand. Determination on my brow, I was ready to fly! Que the slow-motion strut and hypothetical crowd cheering me on. If you're going to do something stupid, you might as well do it in front of a crowd, right?

I inched over to the eight-foot edge of my life's greatest challenge. I am pretty sure my life flashed before my eyes. It was a quick flash, seeing I was only about twelve, but sobering nonetheless. With a quick shuffle of my feet and both hands clasping all four corners of my make-shift parachute, I made a jump for it.

It worked! My plan actually worked!

And by working, I mean I plummeted to the ground with a complete air time of about half a second. I was motionless. I felt a slight ache flow through my body and a strong taste of dirt in my mouth. Ah! the taste of defeat.

I looked down to see the bone sticking out of my broken leg. No, I'm totally kidding. My story isn't that awesome. Believe it or not, I walked away with minor cuts and bruises. My pride, of course, was the greatest wound of all.

What do I want you to see through this story? That I was completely insane? No.

I literally thought in my mind that I was going to fly around the yard using an old beach towel as a parachute. And though that's funny now, back then I really believed it! My heart was convinced it was a probable feat, when in reality, it was completely impossible.

May I burst your bubble for a second? Perfection is impossible. We are finite beings with very limited abilities. No matter how exuberant, educated, or efficient our efforts are, we cannot touch a glimpse of perfection.

That is hard for many of us to swallow. As I mentioned in my Evil Kinevil saga, we actually believe that we can achieve the impossible.

If we could just plan far enough in advance, it would all work out.

If we just believe in our abilities intensely enough, then we will truly be satisfied with the result.

If we could reach perfection, then maybe we would feel like we are worth something of value.

There's a toxic problem with that ideology. The emphasis is all on our own performance. It's all about our ability or feeling of self-worth that drives an unending scurry to be the person we wish we were or live in a reality that is abstractedly impossible. We drive ourselves crazy by the standards we set for ourselves, and restlessness slowly slips in the back door unaware.

According to *Psychology Today*, this kind of thinking "is frequently accompanied by depression, anxiety, obsessive-compulsive disorder, eating disorders, and even suicidal impulses." It is a mentality that can affect your mental and physical well-being and leave you—you guessed it—restless.

Before we get to the heart of this relentless drive, let's take a look at some characteristics of a perfectionist. I am not a medical professional, so this is purely for informational purposes based on my personal experiences. Actually, I just stared in the mirror for twenty minutes and came away with the multiple personalities of a perfectionist. I'll do my best to not write my autobiography here.

The Huff-and-Puffer

You get easily mad or annoyed when something doesn't go your way. Small things send you blowing your top, especially when plans change. It doesn't take much—an off-handed comment or a grumpy co-worker—to put you into a spiral of despair, and a completely ruined day. Everyday issues are just too much to handle, and they have a devastating effect on your emotional and spiritual well-being.

There is a difference in reacting to an inconvenience and responding to it. Perfectionists tend to react to a problem with a self-made plan or brash action. However, Scripture teaches us to have a Holy Spirit response.

Proverbs 14:29 says, *"He that is slow to wrath is of great understanding: but he that is hasty of spirit exalteth folly."*

The Do-It-Yourselfer

You think that when you delegate work to others you are just setting yourself up for disappointment. This can come across to your friends or employees as a micromanager. You have to have your hands on everything because you truly believe it all depends on you. Sometimes this is caused by past mistreatment or unmet expectations of a family member or friend. Either way, you'd rather not chance it.

The Eternalist

You have what I call the Eternal Syndrome. Everything that you put your hand to must have a lasting and eternal effect. On the outset, this looks like a good quality. Why wouldn't you want to live for eternal things, right? True, but when you feel like you always have to do something productive and you literally can't sit still, then it becomes a serious issue.

If you have the eternal syndrome, your mindset is that there is no time for fooling around: life is too short and your mission is too serious. If there is no meaningful end to the task at hand, you would rather just not do it. Wasting time absolutely scares you into oblivion to the point that you get annoyed when someone is distracting you with "meaningless nonsense."

The Absolutist

The Absolutist is an ugly cousin of the eternalist. He usually possesses the all-or-nothing attitude. It's the mindset of "she is mean" versus "she is sometimes mean." You have a habit of

31

labeling people upon one encounter or instance of bad behavior. Yes, you judge a book by its cover.

Playing the martyr is your favorite role when offended. "If they're going to treat me this way, I'm just not going to do anything at all!" You run to the extreme instead of taking things in stride.

The Procrastinator

You were that kid in junior high that would get sick to your stomach at the thought of a Science Fair.

- But what am I going to do?
- Will Susie's project be better than mine?
- Oh, I hope everyone doesn't think it's dumb!

And so, you would sit at home and work and plan and work and plan and work and plan—and never feel like you were ever done. You have what some call "Analysis Paralysis." You think about it so much that you never actually do it, or never end up finishing it. Procrastination seems to be your friend because it might just get you closer to perfection.

This is completely difficult for a perfectionist writer. For instance, like the one you're reading from now. I can't tell you how many times I have had to remind myself to stay focused. If it weren't for an awesome support system of people pushing me ahead, this book would probably not be in print today.

The People Pleaser

We all like to think that we are not the product of someone else's ideals. We are strong, independent people with superpowers that need no sidekicks, right? But the truth is, we often make many of

32

our decisions solely based upon what someone else thinks of us. We check our outfits to make sure they're up to the latest trend before a party with our peers. We drop subtle hints about our accolades in hopes that others will respect us. We constantly analyze what someone else might be thinking about us. We've all been there. But these thoughts and actions make the tried-and-true recipe for anxiety and fear.

It's this perfectionistic mindset that will move you to places you never wanted to go! It will spin your head around into a whirlwind of insecurity, and before you know it, you will start to feel worthless. You'll realize that you can't meet everybody's expectations perfectly. You can't be everybody's superhero. You will ultimately get to the place where you think nobody sees your value and nobody understands you.

So then you'll bow your back and try to be the Do-It-Yourselfer we talked about earlier. You'll work really hard to be considered by your peers as an expert or guru in an effort to earn their respect. You'll take small off-handed comments as a personal attack on your intelligence and eventually convince yourself that you don't need anyone.

The Critic

Perfectionism often leads to being highly critical of yourself and other "go-getters." You tend to focus so much on problems and inefficiencies that they are all you tend to see the moment you walk into a room.

- Do they look better than I do?
- Am I smarter than they are?
- Could I take them in a fight? (Mainly we guys)
- Look what she's wearing!
- Does he know his shirt tale is hanging out?

You're chuckling right now because you know you have had the same thoughts before. Being critical is damaging, not only to your self-confidence but also to those around you. You have placed a blindfold over your eyes refusing to see the good, and it holds you back from developing healthy relationships with others.

***

We see the problem with perfectionism. It is damaging to our mind and soul, and gives way to a crippled life of restlessness. It hinders our hands from the Master's use, and sets expectations that even He does not place on us.

So, if perfectionism is not the answer for rest, then what is?

CHAPTER FOUR

The Dangers of Pleasure

Y ou throw yourself onto your plush seven-foot couch after a long hard day of torrential work overload.

"Ahhh! At last! Some time to unwind!"

You have made a strict resolution to not lift another finger until you have watched at least the first half of the game. You quickly turn on your TV to check the score in hopes that your team is on the upside and...commercial.

"Commercial! Ugh! Why do I pay for this stuff?"

But in your utter exhaustion and complete boredom, you sit there ever-so-still, eyes fixed on the screen.

Have you ever really noticed those commercials? What is the imagery they use all the time to get you to buy? It's usually someone with their hands folded tightly around a warm cup of coffee and a convincing expression of pure bliss as they sit on their newly financed velvet curved loveseat. Or it is someone peacefully lying down on a $4,000 mattress that claims to be the cure-all to sleepers everywhere. Or what about an advertisement for a vacation getaway or grand resort? They say things like,

· "Your calm awaits here!"
· "Where happiness begins."
· "Where problems are far away."

Do you know what they are trying to say? "If you come here or buy this, your problems will all go away and you can finally be at rest." The world paints pictures of rest that are quiet, but not peaceful. They are still, but not satisfying. They are happy, but not full of joy. Peace is sellable. They know you want rest, and they know you are willing to pay the cost. "Advertising is literally an attempt to monetize our restlessness." [9]

But why does this tactic seem to do the trick time and time again? Because you were made for rest and pleasure. God has ingrained in every fiber of our being the desire to Sabbath—rest. And I'm not just talking about *"Remember the sabbath day, to keep it holy,"* (Exodus 20:8) although that is vitally important. I'm talking about the mentality of Sabbath that refreshes our souls and breathes in the constant flow of Christ's enriching peace every day. That is what the world is so desperately trying to imitate. And it's through this God-given desire that we often set our eyes to the skies, hoping the next pleasure will give us a stillness in our soul.

I think a quick glance at our bank statements will tell us where we choose to place our pleasures:

· The average family spends close to $4,800 per year on vacations. [10]

- In a report by West Monroe, "the average consumer spends on average $273 per month on TV streaming subscriptions, home Wifi, mobile phone services, cloud storage, dating apps, ebooks, pet supplies, meal services and the like." [11]
- Statista shows that Americans spent $43.3 billion on video games in 2018. [12]

But what's wrong with a vacation getaway or sitting back and watching the game? What's wrong with checking out for a while to unwind?

Nothing. But I believe that there are droves of people that are trying to buy rest, trying to buy a reset button for life. They are banking on sinful pleasures to gratify their restlessness.

Notice the dangers of pleasure that will come if we listen to our restless hearts.

Distraction

It is my firm conviction that many people run to the pleasures of this world because they simply wish to distract themselves from pain. They live their lives indulging themselves in meaningless distractions that never get to the root of the problem. They buy the knock-off brand of true inner peace and rely on some new-found pleasure to dismiss their troubles. It's the escape-artist mindset that has them scurrying to buy the next plane ticket out from under their responsibilities.

Even the great King David said it this way: *"Oh that I had wings like a dove! for then would I fly away, and be at rest,"* (Psalms 55:6).

He, like many of us, just wanted to run away and avoid responsibility altogether. We unwittingly blame our circumstances for our inability to rest. But we can't forget that restlessness is a matter of the soul, not a matter of our circumstances. Restlessness follows you when you leave town. It follows you when you clock-out. The problem of our restlessness is a root from the inside, not a result from the outside.

I think we often expel so much energy trying to change our circumstance instead of changing ourselves. We do everything in our power to create a perfect environment for rest. Everything has to be perfectly quiet—to-do lists all done, emails cleared, problems settled—before we can be calm.

But what happens when you can't run away? When you can't change your circumstances? It is then that many people start the hunt—the distraction hunt. We reach for a socially acceptable narcotic of choice: scrolling on social media, browsing Amazon, binge-watching a Hulu Original, drowning out the world with music, looking at pornography, etc. Whatever will distract from the pain of today will do—for now. [13]

We have let our restlessness determine the direction of our lives by simply giving in to a distraction. And then we wonder why we can't focus. We are distracted by distractions from distractions. We have settled for a ghost of satisfaction and distracted our lives into an oblivion of unfulfilled purpose. We are simply distracted from God.

Look at these startling statistics on TV usage in America:

- Americans spend an average of five hours and four minutes watching TV every day. (That's approximately nine years of your life!)
- 99% of homes in the U.S. have at least one TV.

- The average household has two TVs.
- 67% of American families watch TV while eating dinner.
- 49% of Americans say they watch too much TV. [14]

Don't you think we are at least a little distracted? Reviews.org did a survey of one thousand Americans, ages eighteen and older, and this is what they found:

- On average, Americans check their phones 262 times per day. (That's once every five and a half minutes!)
- 87.8% feel uneasy leaving their phones at home.
- 55.4% use or look at their phones while driving.
- 75.4% consider themselves addicted to their phones.
- 57.4% say they use their phones on dates.
- 64.2% have texted someone else in the same room.
- 32% of survey respondents say they spend more time on their phones than they do with their spouse.
- 17.3% of parents said they spend more time on their phones than with their children.
- 58% reported that they spend over three hours on their phones each day.
- 65% of people sleep with their phones.
- 70% use their phones on the toilet. [15]

I think it's safe to say we are invariably distracted by our ever-changing world. This is one of the dangers of pleasure. What can be a harmless moment of "checking out" can be the very thing that distracts us from Jesus. But I believe there is a greater danger of pleasure. It is when we let our distractions become the reason for our existence. When once caught our eye becomes the thing that we have placed our dependency on for rest.

Dependency

Our dependency is rooted in our worship. What we put our trust in is ultimately the thing we bow the knee to. Sure, it may seem small and insignificant, but I've seen a small, insignificant pleasure become the altar on which some have sacrificed everything.

- We sacrifice the Lord's Day for travel ball.
- We skip Connect Group for a money-making opportunity.
- We substitute our time with God for time on our phones.
- We sacrifice performance at our main job by obsessing over our "side-hustle."

Our pleasurable distractions have now become our idols. This is why Paul said, *"Wherefore, my dearly beloved, flee from idolatry,"* (I Corinthians 10:14). Idols are the things you turn to instead of Jesus. They are the pleasures you depend on to give you rest for your inner man. They are indeed the objects of your worship.

According to Susanna Wesley, mother of John and Charles Wesley, an idol is "whatever weakens your reason, impairs the tenderness of your conscience, obscures your sense of God, takes off your relish for spiritual things, whatever increases the authority of the body over the mind, that thing is sin to you, however innocent it may seem in itself."

Idols are the enemies of rest and the danger of pleasure. Remember the children of Israel in Exodus 32? Israel, God's chosen people—those He had delivered out of bondage—turned their gaze to an idol. Moses was up on Mt. Sinai for forty days receiving instruction from the Lord. It was in this moment that something changed in the hearts of God's people and compelled them to serve another god.

But how did their worship change so drastically after seeing God do so many great miracles? I think the answer to that question will help us discover why we choose idols instead of Jesus, and place our dependency on pleasure to give us rest.

They were fearful. The monster you choose to let live under your bed will control you. My financial advisor tells me all the time, "There are two things in the world that control the money market: greed and fear. And which one do you think is the strongest emotion?" You guessed it. Fear.

I believe this was the catalyst behind Israel's constructing the golden calf. It was a reaction of fear instead of a response in faith. Exodus 32:1 says, *"...for we wot not what has become of him."*

The person on whom they were dependent for leadership and guidance was gone. There was no sign that Moses was alive. There were no answers—only questions. Their fear of the unknown compelled them to change the course of their worship.

Many people do things they never thought they would by simply listening to their fears. What they thought they would never sacrifice, they have bound and tossed into the fire of their greatest pleasure. But when we place our dependency on our pleasures to give us rest, there will always be a cost.

"And all the people brake off the golden earrings which were in their ears, and brought them unto Aaron," (Exodus 32:3).

Fear will cost you what is truly valuable. I can testify that my greatest moments of fear have been when I lost sight of my Jesus. I made a deliberate choice to take Christ down off the throne and replaced His undying grace for fearful idols. Have you ever thought about how much of God's blessings you have missed out on because you trusted your fears?

The children of Israel let fear blind their worship. Our fears will do the same to us if we let them.

They were forgetful. This part in the story really hits home for me. Not only did they turn their back on God so quickly, but they even gave the credit of their deliverance to a golden statue. Now, the Pharisee in me wants to dispute the fact that I would never do such a thing to Christ, but I know myself all too well. The reality is that none of us are above turning our back on God. Neither were God's chosen people.

"They have turned aside quickly out of the way which I commanded them: they have made them a molten calf, and have worshipped it, and have sacrificed thereunto, and said, These be thy gods, O Israel, which have brought thee up out of the land of Egypt," (Exodus 32:8).

"They forgat God their saviour, which had done great things in Egypt;" (Psalm 106:21).

And it wasn't as if they had gone a long time without seeing the hand of God move for them. Only thirty days had passed since God's appearing to the entire congregation of Israel. They all saw God with their own eyes and yet so quickly wandered from His commandments.

We are all prone to wander—prone to forget what God has done for us. Take yourself back to the moment you first met Him. Do you remember the joy and peace that you had in His presence? Do you remember the exhilaration of Christ's salvation raining in on your restless soul?

What happened? Where did the peace go? Where did the overwhelming grace flee to? Could it be that we have forgotten some things? We have forgotten about His love which first loved us. We have forgotten His grace by which He saved us. We have forgotten His compassion by which He moved to heal us. We have forgotten His blessings that He faithfully bestows on us. We have forgotten His comfort by which He will not leave us comfortless.

We have forgotten God. In a world of distraction and unending pleasure, we have moved our dependency upon the tangible.

Paul speaks to the church of Galatia about this very thing. *"Howbeit then, when ye knew not God, ye did service unto them which by nature are no gods. But now, after that ye have known God, or rather are known of God, how turn ye again to the weak and beggarly elements, whereunto ye desire again to be in bondage?"* (Galatians 4:8-9).

When we seek pleasure outside of the Person of Jesus Christ, we are in essence binding ourselves to the shackles God has delivered us from. We return to the ways of Egypt because we have let the truth of God slip from our minds.

"Therefore we ought to give the more earnest heed to the things which we have heard, lest at any time we should let them slip," (Hebrews 2:1).

They gave in to their flesh. Here comes the hard part in regards to our idols. Idols come in all shapes and sizes. And no, I'm not talking about a statue of Buddha on your front porch. I'm talking about common things that creep their way onto the throne of our lives and become what we live for. Notice the children of Israel:

"And they rose up early on the morrow, and offered burnt offerings, and brought peace offerings; and the people sat down to eat and to drink, and rose up to play," (Exodus 32:6).

Now tell me. What is wrong with eating? Drinking (not alcohol)? Playing? The answer is nothing. Food, drink, and recreation are all basic needs of the human body (flesh). I believe the Holy Spirit is teaching a valuable lesson. When we take something, even out of necessity, and use it for our pleasure instead of Christ's, it has become an idol. There's no coincidence that I Corinthians 10:31 challenges us that *"Whether therefore ye eat, or drink, or whatsoever ye do, do all to the glory of God."*

God wishes to have control of the small things because He knows we can become dependent upon the small things instead of Him. Why do think Christ teaches us to fast? Because when we learn to say no to the desires of our flesh, we have then placed our complete dependence on the Word of God for our meat.

Dietrich Bonhoeffer, a heroic martyr for Christ, shares his battle with his flesh: "With irresistible power desire seizes mastery over the flesh.... It makes no difference whether it is sexual desire, or ambition, or vanity, or desire for revenge, or love of fame and power, or greed for money.... Joy in God is...extinguished in us, and we seek all our joy in the creature. At this moment God is quite unreal to us; He loses all reality, and only desire for the creature is real.... Satan does not here fill us with hatred of God, but with forgetfulness of God.... The lust thus aroused envelops the mind and will of man in deepest darkness. The powers of clear discrimination and of decision are taken from us. The questions present themselves: 'Is what the flesh desires really sin in this case?' 'Is it really not permitted to me, yes — expected of me, now, here, in my particular situation, to appease desire?'... It is here that everything within me rises up against the Word of God." [16]

We can easily convince our flesh that we need something simply because we desire to have it. *"The spirit truly is ready, but the flesh is weak,"* (Mark 14:38b).

Drifting

The last danger of pleasure comes with an extra sneaky nature. In fact, it requires you to do absolutely nothing. That's right! Nothing!

"But wait! I'd love to sit and do nothing! That sounds like a good time to me," say moms of teenagers everywhere.

This is where your picture of rest can become a little muddy. You may want to be the lady in the commercial with the huge cup of coffee on the loveseat or the guy lying in the hammock at the grand resort. Why? Because they are simply doing their favorite thing—nothing.

Just ask my wife. I am really, really good at nothing. I mean, I have an invaluable talent to lock my brain into my "Nothing Box" and throw away the key, if you know what I'm saying. I'm a varsity player when it comes to nothing. But is doing nothing really doing nothing? I'm afraid not. We are always heading somewhere. The wheels are always turning.

It is the same in our spiritual lives. There is no neutral ground where we can pop our discipleship into cruise control and accelerate to a closer walk with Jesus. There is no setting the sails once in order to get to where Jesus wants us to go. We are either following Christ's direction for our lives, or we are drifting.

Drift means "a gradual shift in position; an aimless course; to become carried along subject to no guidance or control." We cannot and will not drift our way to holiness or spiritual maturity. We are subject to the winds and waves of worldly culture.

D. A. Carson says, "People do not drift toward holiness. Apart from grace-driven effort, people do not gravitate toward godliness, prayer, obedience to Scripture, faith, and delight in the

Lord. We drift toward compromise and call it tolerance; we drift toward disobedience and call it freedom; we drift toward superstition and call it faith. We cherish the indiscipline of lost self-control and call it relaxation; we slouch toward prayerlessness and delude ourselves into thinking we have escaped legalism; we slide toward godlessness and convince ourselves we have been liberated.... We cherish the indiscipline of lost self-control and call it relaxation." [17]

Drifting is the only destination of the one who lives for pleasure. But why do we drift so easily? How do we drift so far from Jesus without even realizing it?

Many times, I believe we drift because we have not defined our God-given purpose. You just read it. Drifting is an "aimless course." There is no bullseye. There is not a destination. There is no purpose. Charles Stanley said, "When we lack direction, we don't simply stagnate. We continue to move, usually in an unhealthy direction."

Your direction and your purpose go hand-in-hand. You can't have one without the other. If you know your purpose in life, then you will know what will give you pleasure along the way. You won't live in distraction because there will be one set focus. You will not live dependent upon your idols for satisfaction because your worship will be Christ alone. You will not easily drift because you have defined your direction. [18]

So, let me start in the obvious place. What is your purpose? You woke up with breath in your lungs today—why? Why has God given you life? You have to answer that question. It's not a gimmie. When you have answered why you are here, you will know which pleasures have to go. You will know what must be taken out of your life so that rest may find its proper place.

The dangers of pleasure are real. We can become distracted from God while doing all the right things. We can become dependent upon our idols to exalt us to a place of rest. We can drift far from Jesus with something as simple as a whimsical desire.

But praise be to God, Jesus has made a way for our souls to be quiet! He has given us the merit for peace that puts to shame the lies of the world, the flesh, and the devil, and silences all the results of a restless heart.

PART TWO

The **Remedy** for **Restlessness**

CHAPTER FIVE

The Person of Rest

"Come unto me…"

My wife and I love having guests in our home. It is a very special time that we can get to know the people in our church and show them some good 'ole southern hospitality. Extending an invitation to someone is a special thing. In essence you are saying, "Come be a part of who I am and what I am doing." You value the individuals enough to bring them into your life and open wide your heart to them. You go out of your way to make preparation for the visit an accommodate your guests with the best you have to offer.

In return, when that invitation is accepted, your guests will be the beneficiary of your life and home. They will be able to check out from their own troubles and just enjoy your fellowship for a while. And then, when they finally arrive, you scold yourself for even worrying over having everything just perfect. Why? Because the preparation now seems menial compared to the sweet fellowship that you enjoy with one another.

My friends, the moment has come. The preparations have been made. Rest for your soul invites you to come near. But it is not a ticket to a vacation resort. It doesn't come with a 401K. And it certainly doesn't look like a brand-new car. Then what does soul rest look like?

It looks like Jesus.

You see, our rest is found in Someone, not something. There is nothing under the sun that can substitute what Jesus alone can do for you. It is through coming to Christ that you are merited calmness and serenity. He has made the preparations at Calvary, and *"who for the joy that was set before him endured the cross, despising the shame, and is set down at the right hand of the throne of God,"* (Hebrews 12:2). He bids us to come to Him for our rest and peace, not to the things of the world.

We have seen what happens when we believe the lies of culture that prosperity is the answer to our problems. We expel all of our energy to accumulate more stuff and live in search for the land of ER. We try to get all we can in hopes that it will leave us satisfied. And when the day is done and the dollar is spent, we turn into our beds having nothing left to give Jesus. Our bodies are still and all is quiet, but our souls are crying.

Jesus is pleading with you. He wants you to come to Him and keep on coming day after day. He wants to fellowship with you and to be intricately connected to every aspect of your life—your home, school, job, etc. He wants to fellowship with you every moment that you will give Him. He doesn't want to be forgotten when you go to work. He does not want to leave when you go out with your friends. He wants you.

Remember when Christ turned to a fisherman named Peter, and bid him, *"Follow me"*? His urging did not stop there. While on the sea of Galilee, in the midst of a tempestuous storm, Christ's invitation to Peter was much the same: *"Come,"* (Matthew 14:29). It was a simplistic cry for intimacy and surrender. It was an extension of grace that pulled a man out of trouble and gave him anchoring faith. Imagine what Peter would have missed if he had rejected Christ's invitation!

You may think that the waves of a reckless soul keep crashing into you, and there is no way out. The storm has beaten you, and Christ is nowhere to be found. But look beyond the troubled waters of your circumstances and see Christ walking on the water toward you. All trouble, all restlessness—they're all under His feet. He is not focused on the waves or the winds, but on you.

Again, to the weary soul He says, *"Come unto me..."*

In the context of Matthew 11, this was a very timely message. Christ was speaking to a group of some seventy followers that had been laboring in Jerusalem and had seen God's hand beginning to work. This is why He said, *"Come unto me, all ye that labour and are heavy laden."* It was an invitation to all that were around Him to come to be the beneficiary of all that He is and does. In essence He was saying, "Stop going, and start coming."

Christ is teaching that rest never comes in pursuit of it. Rest is not the goal; God is the goal. When you connect your life to the person of Jesus, you grow deeper into His character, and rest becomes a by-product of abiding in Him.

It is the same in our relationships with others, isn't it? I can joyfully say that I know more about my wife today than I did when we first started dating. Why? Because I have spent much time in her presence. Our lives have been connected on every level. As a result, I have learned what she likes and dislikes, and my love for her has grown exponentially. It is a constant pursuit of each other that leads to a bedrock of trust.

Christ, in essence, says to us, "Pursue me." The more we know His person—Who He is—the more we can come into His rest and be assured that He is enough. Nothing more. Nothing less. Prosperity is not rest. Relief is not rest. Jesus is your rest. So, let's go deeper into Who Christ is and, by doing so, we will learn how to rest.

He Is Compassionate

"And Jesus, when he came out, saw much people, and was moved with compassion toward them, because they were as sheep not having a shepherd: and he began to teach them many things," (Mark 6:34).

I believe we often do not find rest for our souls because we believe Jesus does not care. We think he is not touched with the feeling of our infirmities, and He does not wish to relieve us of our misery.

Is it possible that the disciples thought the same thing while on the boat in the middle of the storm? I think so. Their circumstances blinded them from remembering Who He was and how much He cared.

Remember the little children in Mark 3? The disciples were getting annoyed at those "bothersome kids" trying to crowd around Jesus. The disciples ordered them to be quiet or to go away. But the children sensed Jesus' heart was full of love for them and waited with anticipation to be held tightly in His loving embrace. After Jesus bid them to come to Him, He prayed God's hand of blessing on them. Later, He rebuked His disciples' reactions and taught them that if one wished to enter into the kingdom of God, he must come as a child: teachable, humble, believing.

Remember the lepers that Jesus did not turn away in Matthew 8:1-4? He was not at all afraid to go to those men whose bodies were filled with this infectious disease and touch that that they might be healed. Lepers were the outcasts of society in Jesus' day. No one wanted anything to do with them. But God, rich in mercy, reached down to the lowest of lows to heal the souls that had been troubled by sin's curse.

And what about the man for whom the world saw no hope, the Maniac of Gadara (Mark 5:1-20)? Jesus made a special trip to see a man possessed with many devils. Upon His arrival, the maniac saw Jesus afar off *"and cried with a loud voice, and said, What have I to do with thee, Jesus, thou Son of the most high God? I adjure thee by God, that thou torment me not."* But Jesus had compassion on the man and delivered his soul from the evil spirits.

And what about the restless soul in our world today? What about you? Do you see yourself in the child that is in dire need of His love or in the leper that must be cleansed and made whole? Do you see yourself high on the mountain of a restless world, desperate for anything to cut the chains and release the enemy that steals your rest?

But Jesus. He is our friend. He is compassionate to all the weary and heavy laden. He will not turn you away.

When we know how much He cares, we will not deny His rest. Hebrews 4:14-16 says, *"Seeing then that we have a great high priest, that is passed into the heavens, Jesus the Son of God, let us hold fast our profession. For we have not an high priest which cannot be touched with the feeling of our infirmities; but was in all points tempted like as we are, yet without sin. Let us therefore come boldly unto the throne of grace, that we may obtain mercy, and find grace to help in time of need."*

We can come boldly into His presence and there learn something of rest!

His compassion says, *"Come unto me..."*

He Is Consistent

Isn't it amazing how time changes us? It heals us, helps us grow, and turns our perspectives. Just think what life was like ten years prior to this moment. Do you look any different? Do you have different aspirations and goals?

Did you know that Jesus, Who has promised us rest, has never changed? He is not more mature today than He was "back then." He has no more room to grow. For Him, there are no reminiscing of the good ole days. *"Jesus Christ the same yesterday, and today, and for ever," (Hebrews 13:8).*

In a world of uncertainty, our God is certain of what He wants for you! Although change comes to rear its ugly head and scrambles our lives to pieces, we can rest in the fact that our Savior never changes.

Charles Spurgeon encouraged a group of believers who had experienced great disappointments: "Some of you have come here childless, or widows, or fatherless, still weeping your recent affliction. Changes have taken place in your estate that have made your heart full of misery. Your cups of sweetness have been dashed with draughts of gall; your golden harvests have had tares cast into the midst of them, and you have had to reap the noxious weed along with the precious grain. Your much fine gold has become dim, and your glory has departed; the sweet frames at the commencement of last year became bitter ones at the end. Your raptures and your ecstacies were turned into depression and forebodings. Alas! for our changes, and hallelujah to Him that hath no change." [19]

This crazy world can't change our God or His message. *"His truth endureth to all generations,"* (Psalm 100:5). When we truly grasp that our God does not alter from His original state, we can breathe in the surety of His rest, and let it refresh our weary souls!

> *If today He deigns to bless us*
> *With a sense of pardoned sin,*
> *He to-morrow may distress us,*
> *Make us feel the plague within.*
> *All to make us*
> *Sick of self and fond of Him.*
>
> *Immutable His will,*
> *Though dark may be my frame,*
> *His loving heart is still*
> *Unchangeably the same.*
> *My soul through many changes goes,*
> *His love no variation knows.* [20]

His consistency says, *"Come unto me..."*

He Is Close

One of the greatest honors God has given me in life is fatherhood. At this time, He has blessed Kathryn and me with a precious little girl named Lilly and adorable twins, Trevor and Annabelle. Lilly is the exuberant bundle of sunshine that smiles all the time. I prayed when we were expecting her that God would give us a happy baby, and God graciously answered my request—and then some. She is the happiest little girl I have ever seen and adds a spirit to our home like no other.

But even with pink dresses, big bows, and eyes that will melt you, there is still a lot of fight in that girl. Don't let the long eyelashes fool you. She is a tough little cookie that knows how to hold her own against three boy cousins.

I remember one of the first times that I noticed her relentlessness. I was doing what dads do best: trying to rock her to sleep. To her defense, she had had a long day of fun and was not having any part of this night-night stuff. As I sat down in my chair, she began to wiggle violently like a fish on the seashore. It was everything I could do to keep her in my arms and both of us from flying out of the chair. I immediately began to get frustrated.

Why can't you just go to sleep?

This is going to take all night!

It's amazing how your kids show you how selfish you really are. After several minutes of this happy parade, I looked at my wife with this "I don't think it's going to work" expression.

In her gentle, motherly tone she said, "Talk to her, Daddy." With an eye-roll and furrowed brow, I tried my best to control my irritation and talk soothingly to Lilly. It helped a little, but she was still so restless. After praying and asking God to forgive me of my selfish attitude, I just continued to reassure her that Daddy and Mommy love her, and that it was okay to go to sleep.

I remember holding her tightly, not so that it would hurt her, but tightly enough so that she would not fall out of my arms. Not long after this persistent embrace and reassurance, she stopped kicking and whining; and her body settled down. With a whispered "goodnight" and a few gentle kisses on the head, our little girl was fast asleep.

God taught me a valuable lesson that day. I am so much like Lilly and so little like my Jesus. I kick and scream when I don't get my way. I get fed up with the burdens that I carry, and restlessly fuss at God that He is nowhere to be found. And all the while, He holds me tightly and reassures me that all things work together for good. I kick against His hands and think He's trying to hurt me, but His compassion and consistency hold me close so that I do not fall from His loving embrace.

The instance with my daughter that day reminded me of the famous poem "Footprints in the Sand" by Carolyn Joyce Carty.

One night a man had a dream.
He dreamed he was walking along the beach with the Lord.
Across the sky flashed scenes from his life.
For each scene, he noticed two sets of footprints in the sand:
One belonging to him, and the other to the Lord.

When the last scene of his life flashed before him,
He looked back at the footprints in the sand.
He noticed that many times along the path of his life there was
only one set of footprints.
He also noticed that it happened at the very lowest and saddest
times in his life.
This really bothered him and he questioned the Lord about it.

"Lord, You said that once I decided to follow you,
You'd walk with me all the way.
But I have noticed that during the most troublesome times in my
life,
There is only one set of footprints.

I don't understand why, when I needed You most, You would leave me."

The Lord replied,
"My son, My precious child, I love you and I would never leave you.
During your times of trial and suffering,
When you see only one set of footprints,
It was then that I Carried You."

When I finally believe His words and stop kicking against His hands, it is then that I can rest. I just crawl up in His arms and face the fact that I can't take it. I am too weak. I am too prone to wander, prone to leave the God I love. I must break away all ties with the world. I must come close, for that is all that He desires.

His closeness says, *"Come unto me…"*

***

His compassion, consistency, and closeness are lifting their voices to our noisy soul, reminding us that He is the answer to our rest. So why do we push Him away? We know that He loves us. We know that He wants to fellowship with us. So why do we have such a hard time coming into His presence to find rest? Is it because we are afraid? Maybe we fear coming to Him because we don't know what it will cost. We are afraid of what He might take away or what He might ask us to place on the altar of surrender. We are scared to death of the thought that the comfy securities we have held onto so tightly, might just be torn from our grasp if we obey His voice. It's as if we feel He is an intruder that is waiting for the opportunity to rob us of our wealth and dismantle our lives. But is this truly the heart of Christ?

King David said, *"Search me, O God, and know my heart: try me, and know my thoughts: And see if there be any wicked way in me, and lead me in the way everlasting,"* (Psalm 139:23-24). David gave God a full search warrant into his life. His heart was open, his mind focused on God. He understood that openness and transparency with God would usher in the fulness of His presence and bring peace in the midst of trouble. And if anyone knew trouble, it was King David. Sometimes it was a self-inflicted trouble. Psalm 38:3 says, *"There is no soundness in my flesh because of thine anger; neither is there any rest in my bones because of my sin,"* (Psalm 38:3). Other times, it was an invasion of the enemy towards God's people. Either way, David knew that rest began the moment He got honest with God.

Come to Him. Do not hide from His compassion. Do not doubt His consistency. Do not push away from His closeness. Come and find rest unto your soul.

CHAPTER SIX

The Privilege of Rest

"...and I will give you rest..."

There is no day like payday. The rush of landing a huge client or receiving a few weeks' reward for your hard work is always satisfying. It constitutes a deep feeling of worth when you know you did your job well, and you received a good reward. So, you strut your way to the bank with your "millions" in your pocket, and you come home with a bag filled with so much money, you don't know what to do with it all! Right? Well, maybe not quite like that.

It is a great tragedy though that many of us use this same ideology when it comes to the restlessness within. Heartache suddenly interrupts our way of life, so we either bury our head in the sand or just try to push through, hoping to somehow find rest for our soul. Our knees become feeble from all of life's responsibilities, and we just hope "payday" will come soon. "Maybe if I work hard now, everything will get better later! The grass is always greener on the other side, right?"

We have seen what the result of toxic productivity does to the mind and body. It depletes us of our senses and strips our ability to be present. Our emotions become a machine, and before we know it, our accomplishments become a meaningless pursuit that somehow doesn't "do the trick." We bear the notion that our hard labor and religious achievements have given us a warrant for rest. We are deceived into a "persuasive violence" of the body and soul. Yes, we have passion for what we do, but we are an addict to the work of our hands.

But we must not overlook the words Christ uses in this passage. He said, *"Come unto me all ye that labour and are heavy laden, and I will give you rest,"* (Matthew 11:28).

You don't earn rest.

You cannot expect it upon wishing for it.

You don't receive it through spiritual osmosis.

Soul rest is given to you by the only One that has the means to do so. I bring you back once more to the first three words, *"Come unto me."*

Then Jesus says something quite unusual. *"Take my yoke upon you."* That's a little oxymoronic, don't you think? Jesus just promised us that He would give us rest for our souls, and now He wants us to take on an instrument of work. The yoke was a wooden tool used to hitch two oxen to the same plow. They would work side-by-side for the same purpose of carrying the load.

This picture of taking on Jesus' yoke was significant for more reasons than one. First of all, there were Pharisees in the crowd He was speaking to that day. They considered themselves slaves to law, under the yoke of the Torah. Can you imagine their facial expressions when Jesus looked at them and basically said, "Drop everything you have ever known, get in My yoke, and follow Me"? There is no doubt He got a few questioning looks.

The Pharisees were blinded by their legalism; they put all of their emphasis on what they did rather than for Whom they did it. Their labor in the law was the idol that blinded their hearts them from the grace that Jesus offered.

Secondly, this was a rather confusing thing for the other people standing around Him. Remember there were seventy followers that had just been laboring for Jesus in the ripe fields of Jerusalem (Luke 10). They were worn out, tired from all the right things. And Jesus told them to take on a yoke in order to receive rest.

What! Are you kidding me? But why a yoke? How about a vacation or getaway?

Jesus was trying to teach them that rest can come even in the midst of their labor. He is teaching us the same. Your soul can be at peace even when your mind and body are spent. Look closely. He says, *"My yoke."* It's not your yoke; it's His! It's not your burden; it's His. You are not in competition with Him. You are a co-laborer with Him in one mind and one heart, striving together for the same goal.

Many believers are frustrated because they are trying to pull the burden on their own. I heard a preacher once say that some Christians are carrying burdens God never intended for them to carry.

And all the while, He patiently waits as we put down our plans, dreams, and busy schedule to carry only one burden—His. He wants us to get into the yoke and let Him lead. Saving the world is His job, not ours.

Here are a few principles that will help us channel our drive to be productive and accept Christ's gift of rest in the middle of our labor.

Work Is a Gift from God

We have seen from the beginning that God gifted man with work.

"And the LORD God took the man, and put him into the garden of Eden to dress it and to keep it," (Genesis 2:15).

Work is not always fun, but it is a necessary part of human life. It is beneficial for your health and well-being. It challenges you and gives you the means to develop yourself. It strengthens you socially and psychologically. It provides you with the produce of your labor, whether that be money or something else. As a believer, your work is the witness of your identity in Christ and His purpose for your life.

Colossians 1:10-12 reminds us, *"That ye might walk worthy of the Lord unto all pleasing, being fruitful in every good work, and increasing in the knowledge of God; Strengthened with all might, according to his glorious power, unto all patience and longsuffering with joyfulness; Giving thanks unto the Father, which hath made us meet to be partakers of the inheritance of the saints in light:"*

God wants you to be fruitful. He wants you to worship Him through your work and give it all you've got. The problem comes when we place our identity in the work itself. We let a job define who we are. We let our work schedule control our time. We worship the product instead of a Person. Do you realize that God did not give you the job that you have just to make money? I know this is a revolutionary idea, but your job does not constitute who you are. Many people are tricked into believing that the only hope for rest is dealt on the table of what they can produce. It becomes all about what they can do rather than what He can do. This is oftentimes why some people have a problem with their value. If they are not producing something of value, they deem themselves unworthy. But although we are known by what we do, we are valued by what Christ has already done. This is exactly why our identity and value are solely in Him and not what we can produce.

Think on this passage: *"Ye have not chosen me, but I have chosen you, and ordained you, that ye should go and bring forth fruit, and that your fruit should remain: that whatsoever ye shall ask of the Father in my name, he may give it you,"* (John 15:16).

So, if God ordained you for work, don't you think He will make a way so that you can rest in that work? In the busyness of a hectic day, God can put stillness into your soul—the breath of fresh air that calms every bit of your mind. You will not have to work your fingers to the bone to prove your worth. You will simply be *"confident of this very thing, that he which hath begun a good work in you will perform it until the day of Jesus Christ,"* (Philippians 1:6).

The Lord Does Not Forget That We Need Sleep

I don't know about you, but I love my sleep. I am the guy that absolutely hated all-nighters and New Year's Eve activities. Why? Because it messed with my sleep and made me feel like I had been hit by a Mack truck! Jesus often reminds me that He has not forgotten of my physical need of rest. We have talked a lot about rest for our souls, but it is obvious that we need sleep so that our minds and bodies can recuperate and reenergize. At the end of a taxing work week, or after staying up all night with the kids, God will not forget that sleep is a necessity for you.

David reminds us, *"It is vain for you to rise up early, to sit up late, to eat the bread of sorrows: for so he giveth his beloved sleep,"* (Psalm 127:2).

Sometimes we think Jesus forgets we are human. We think He continues to ask us to do things that we simply just don't have the time or energy for. *"Can a woman forget her sucking child that she should not have compassion on the son of her womb? yea they may forget, yet will I not forget thee,"* (Isaiah 49:15).

God is saying that it is easier for a nursing mother to forget her child than it is for our Heavenly Father to forget us. He has formed us for the work that He calls us to do, and He will take everything into account. He knows your limits. Maybe the reality is that you don't.

It Is Good to Want to Please the Lord with Your Work

There are many people that work their fingers to the bone because they are seeking to please somebody. Sometimes it is pleasing themselves with the ecstasy of building their own empire, but many times it is an attempt to be noticed by those whom they revere.

It's the little kid in all of us that builds an elaborate block tower just so Mommy will be proud. We want Daddy to be watching when we score our first run on the little league team. There's just something about our nature that wants to be seen and heard. Sometimes this is due to problems or trauma from the past.

We have been criticized, so we seek constant assurance that we are doing the things right.

We have been neglected, so we seek acceptance from everyone we meet.

You've heard the phrase: "That person is a people-pleaser." Yep! That's us. We are restless, trying to construct a life someone else would be pleased with.

But did you know it is good to want to please the Lord with our work? *"No man that warreth entangleth himself with the affairs of this life; that he may please him who hath chosen him to be a soldier,"* (II Timothy 2:4).

I think many believers want the rest that Jesus offers but are still entangled with the affairs of this life. They work to please men and not God. Paul said, *"For do I now persuade men, or God? or do I seek to please men? for if I yet pleased men, I should not be the servant of Christ,"* (Galatians 1:10).

God has enabled you to work for His pleasure, not just for your profit. *"Servants, be obedient to them that are your masters according to the flesh, with fear and trembling, in singleness of your heart, as unto Christ; Not with eye service, as menpleasers; but as the servants of Christ, doing the will of God from the heart,"* (Ephesians 6:5-6).

The desire to please is God-given. True rest comes when we realize that work is from Him and should be done to please Him. Whom are you trying to please?

There Is Power in No-thing

What is God's greatest resource? What is His most valuable tool? The answer is—nothing. Literally, NO thing. Our God is the all-sufficient One, the Alpha and Omega. He is the only Hope and the last Amen. He doesn't need our help to get the job done. Instead, He chooses to use our "nothingness" to create something truly beautiful in our lives. He makes beauty from the ashes (Isaiah 61:3), and through our weakness He is made strong (II

Corinthians 12:8-10). When we empty ourselves of ourselves, then God can fill us with love, joy, and—you guessed it—peace. It is the fruit of walking in the Holy Spirit's way and allowing God's creation of righteousness to manifest itself in our lives.

Remember the commencement of God's physical creation? What was on His tool belt? Nothing. All that was required was an emptiness of opportunity and a whisper of love, and "it was good."

There is great power in realizing that you are not enough. Jesus says, *"Abide in me, and I in you. As the branch cannot bear fruit of itself, except it abide in the vine; no more can ye, except ye abide in me. I am the vine, ye are the branches: He that abideth in me, and I in him, the same bringeth forth much fruit: for without me ye can do nothing,"* (John 15:4-5).

That is why He says to come to Him, and He will give us rest. We cannot go get it on our own. We must cut away all of self so that *"He might have the preeminence,"* (Colossians 1:18). In and of yourself, you don't have what it takes to pastor your church as Christ would see fit. You don't have the makeup to nurture your kids in the admonition of the Lord. These are works of God, so they must be fueled by His power and not your own. God only gives rest to those who allow Him to give it. They come empty, broken, so that God may fill them.

Notice the power of nothing in our salvation. There is nothing within us that can make us holy. There is nothing that we can do hard enough or efficiently enough to earn our salvation. Salvation, like soul rest, is a gift from God.

"For by grace are ye saved through faith; and that not of yourselves: it is the gift of God: Not of works, lest any man should boast. For we are his workmanship, created in Christ Jesus unto

good works, which God hath before ordained that we should walk in them," (Ephesians 2:8-10).

There is no work that you or I can do to satisfy a righteous God. There is no job suitable enough. And there is no merit of salvation through our accomplishments. Salvation is not in tradition. It is not from financial contributions to the church. It is not confession to the Pope. Regeneration belongs to Him Who has paid the price with His life on the cross! You bring the dirty vessel, but God does the washing.

Notice the power of nothing in our steps. There is great liberty in letting God control your steps. *"The steps of a good man are ordered by the Lord: and he delighteth in His way,"* (Psalm 37:23). When we realize we don't have all the answers and we cannot lean to our own understanding, then God can truly have His way with us.

I have counseled teenagers who want to have peace about a big decision—a big step—but they are still trying to control the details. They want Jesus to take the wheel, but they still have a firm grip on their lives, hoping to keep some control. When you come to Jesus, you relinquish your control. Your life becomes hidden in Christ and authored by His divine pen.

God stretches out His unseen hand
To endow a precious mark,
To write His script upon earthly vessels
That never shall depart.

Notice the power of nothing in our strength. *"And Jacob was left alone; and there wrestled a man with him until the breaking of the day. And when he saw that he prevailed not against him, he touched the hollow of his thigh; and the hollow of Jacob's thigh was out of joint, as he wrestled with him. And he* *said, Let me go, for the day breaketh. And he said, I will not let thee go, except thou bless me. And he said unto him, What is thy name? And he said, Jacob. And he said, Thy name shall be called no more Jacob, but Israel: for as a prince hast thou power with God and with men, and hast prevailed. And Jacob asked him, and said, Tell me, I pray thee, thy name. And he said, Wherefore is it that thou dost ask after my name? And he blessed him there. And Jacob called the name of the place Peniel: for I have seen God face to face, and my life is preserved. And as he passed over Penuel the sun rose upon him, and he halted upon his thigh. Therefore the children of Israel eat not of the sinew which shrank, which is upon the hollow of the thigh, unto this day: because he touched the hollow of Jacob's thigh in the sinew that shrank,"* (Genesis 32:24-32).

It is amazing how much we wrestle with a God Who knows everything. In all of eternity, Jacob could have never won a wrestling match with God; and yet he wrestled until daybreak. Fighting with God is not a battle that you can win. We may be hard-headed and strong-willed, but our strength will never outlast God's strength. When we bring ourselves low enough, and admit that we cannot win, then Christ can begin to work. Through our weakness He is made strong.

There is no greater example of this than when Christ endured the cross. Through His submission, He satisfied the wrath of a holy God, achieved the glorious resurrection, and conquered death, hell, and the grave. His greatest display of weakness was His highest honor indicative of His deity.

"And he said unto me, My grace is sufficient for thee: for my strength is made perfect in weakness. Most gladly therefore will I rather glory in my infirmities, that the power of Christ may rest upon me. Therefore I take pleasure in infirmities, in reproaches,

in necessities, in persecutions, in distresses for Christ's sake: for when I am weak, then am I strong," (II Corinthians 12:9-10).

Could it be that through our weaknesses God is trying to make Himself strong? To gain the power of your mind and heart and bring about pleasure in your trial. Your weakness may be your greatest asset to God. Let Him use it.

Oh, what a gift that Christ gives to the weary soul! He blesses us with divine work and nourishes our famished bodies. And if that isn't enough, He provides a rest that outlasts any trouble. We don't have to earn it, just accept it. He bids us to come closer, and supplies everything our heart needs.

CHAPTER SEVEN

The Process of Rest

"...and learn of me; ..."

I would argue, that one of the most malleable places for the human mind is found in the classroom. The average person spends most of his childhood being shaped by great stories, science experiments, and vast libraries. And I believe one of the greatest influences in the classroom is not so much the material as it is the one delivering it—the teacher.

Teachers have one of the most challenging jobs in the world as they relay information and pray that just some of it will touch the heart strings and become the anthem of their pupils. Teachers must be creative in their execution of taking the most menial concepts and shaping them into formative value for their students. Their goal is to be individual and inspiring to every young man or woman that seeks to learn. And a teacher that can do all these things well has left a lasting mark on the next generation.

When it comes to our soul rest, Christ is the ultimate teacher. He is ready and willing to pour His heart into the hungry soul that wants Him. He says, *"learn of me."*

Do you see the progression? First, He says, *"Come,"* then *"take,"* and now *"learn."* Finding rest is a process. But there comes a big problem. We don't like things that take time. As one preacher put it, "We all want the product instead of the process." Learning takes too much time and effort—too much heartache and possible disappointment.

Why can't it be instantaneous? Jesus gives us rest. We keep it. Done.

But remember who is also in the yoke with Jesus? You! Soul rest is a process because we are imperfect creatures that require continual work. Sure, we'd like to think our self-imposed standards of perfection will immediately give us rest for our soul, but Jesus doesn't work that way.

We have seen that the life of a perfectionist gets us nowhere fast. We become irritable. We procrastinate on everything. We fear failure constantly. And we are our worst critic. We literally set standards for ourselves to earn the favor God has already given us. Why do we do this to ourselves? Honestly, I think it's because we like to be our own teachers. We take the role of the schoolmaster and think that we can "self-help" our way out of this restless cycle we are trapped in. Introspection can only take you so far. When it comes to your rest, you need divine intervention from the One Who has already learned the lesson.

When we get in the yoke, we begin to learn the lessons necessary to stay in His rest—to *"keep our hearts and minds through Christ Jesus,"* (Philippians 4:7). What are the lessons to be learned from the yoke? He tells us: *"learn of me; for I am meek and lowly in heart:"*

Meek means gentle, mild, and humble. It was the central characteristic of Christ's ministry, and it infiltrated everything He did.

"Gentleness or meekness is the opposite of self-assertiveness and self-interest. It stems from trust in God's goodness and control over the situation. The gentle person is not occupied with self at all. This is a work of the Holy Spirit, not of the human will." [21]

But why does He want to teach us meekness and lowliness? Because one of the greatest enemies of our rest is our pride. It is the monster of self that peers its ugly head from a deceitful heart, and sucks every ounce of spiritual life out of us. Your greatest hurdle to soul rest is not your circumstances. It's not your time management. It's not your job or your finances. It's not your responsibilities. It's not revenge on the person that hurt you. It's not even the burden of the yoke. It is you. The person you look at in the mirror does not want the best for your soul and seeks only to be your schoolmaster.

"The heart is deceitful above all things, and desperately wicked: who can know it?" (Jeremiah 17:9). Your heart will lie to you if you let it. It will convince you that taking on the yoke and learning of Jesus is an act only for those that are of the highest Christian regard. It will fancy the privilege of joining with Jesus, and with chin held high, it will come into the yoke only seeking the blessing not the Blesser. Self tells us, "We will stay if only our needs are met. If only we can be assured of peace. If only Christ will promise us that the future will be easy from this point forward. We will come only if there is room enough for ourselves and the world."

We cannot come to the yoke with our preconditions. We cannot come by our own terms. It is a reckless abandon into a journey with Jesus—no strings attached.

By Jesus' teaching us His meekness, He is demonstrating what we must learn in order to find rest continually. There are two foundational principles of Christ's meekness. They are not easy lessons to learn but are necessary for *"the peace of God, which passeth all understanding,"* (Philippians 4:7).

Suffering

"Okay, I'm done! First, I have to drop everything to follow Jesus and now I am promised suffering in order to find soul rest!" That was my initial reaction. But then I was reminded how everything in life revolves around suffering.

Suffering is a necessity for freedom and the gateway to change. Think of it. It takes a man endowed with bravery to fight until death for the freedoms of others. It is through the strain of vigorous toil and sweat that one becomes strong and able. It is through restless growing pains that a child develops into an independent person, ready to tackle the responsibilities of life.

Suffering is a part of life—especially a life following Jesus. In fact, we are not promised the riches of the world or great fame but we are assured of suffering and affliction. *"Yea, and all that will live godly in Christ Jesus shall suffer persecution,"* (II Timothy 3:12).

We often see suffering pictured in Scripture as a wilderness. The wilderness served as a place of wandering, thirst, hunger, hiding, communion, and death. It was a picture of life outside of comfortable—outside of normal. But when we look at the life of Jesus, He practically lived there. Outside of others' expectations.

Outside of others' comfort zones. It was common place for Him. Many times in His ministry, He separated Himself, and went into the desert to pray and fast.

Luke 4:1 says, *"And Jesus being full of the Holy Ghost returned from Jordan, and was led by the Spirit into the wilderness."*

I think it's important to note that the Holy Ghost was the one Who led Him into the wilderness. Sometimes I think we give the devil too much credit for what God is bringing about in our lives. You've heard it said, "God will never put more on you than you can handle." I don't think that's true at all. I believe God will not put more on you than *He* can handle. Valleys are nothing to the One Who made the mountains.

I think another note to make about this passage is to see who met Jesus in the wilderness—the devil. The devil is that old sly fox who peeks his head up in the wilderness and seeks to devour easy prey. We are ignorant if we think the devil will not meet us in the wilderness experiences of life. These are times when our emotions, body, and will are tired and worn out; and the devil is looking for weak prey—restless prey.

"Be sober, be vigilant; because your adversary the devil, as a roaring lion, walketh about, seeking whom he may devour:" (I Peter 5:8).

Suffering brings pain, but through pain there is great power. Notice Paul's desire in the face of suffering: *"That I may know him, and the power of his resurrection, and the fellowship of his sufferings, being made conformable unto his death;"* (Philippians 3:10).

When you join into the suffering of Jesus—rejection, persecution, heartache—you experience the power of His glorious resurrection and you learn something of Him. It is through the valley—not around, not over, or under—but *through* the valley that you see the wonders of the Shepherd (Psalm 23:4).

Have you ever thought about how Jesus, who was about to face the awful pains of the crucifixion, was at complete rest in His soul? How? Because His faith was anchored in the character of God, not the cares of His circumstances.

Elizabeth Elliot said, "I am not a theologian or a scholar, but I am very aware of the fact that pain is necessary to all of us. In my own life, I think I can honestly say that out of the deepest pain has come the strongest conviction of the presence of God and the love of God."

God becomes real in times of hurt, because you realize He is the only one that can mend the wounds and erase the scars. A verse I find great comfort from in the middle of painful circumstances is II Corinthians 4:15, "*For all things are for your sakes, that the abundant grace might through the thanksgiving of many redound [overflow] to the glory of God.*"

When others see strength amidst your pain, they give thanks to healer and turn their eyes to His glory. That is what it means to live in the yoke. Sometimes it is work, sweat, and pain, but the joy that comes through the suffering is worth the journey with Jesus.

"But rejoice, inasmuch as ye are partakers of Christ's sufferings; that, when his glory shall be revealed, ye may be glad also with exceeding joy. If ye be reproached for the name of Christ, happy are ye; for the spirit of glory and of God resteth upon you: on their part he is evil spoken of, but on your part he is glorified," (I Peter 4:13-14).

Selflessness

A strange thing happened when I read Jesus' words in Matthew 11:29. I did not think about a yoke as the one we described in the last chapter. My mind went back to Jesus' trip to Calvary, when a man named Simon of Cyrene was called to come along Christ and help bear His cross. The Bible doesn't clearly say if they held the cross together or if Simon carried it alone, but here is the visual that comes to mind. Imagine. Two men with a wooden vessel on their back, moving together toward one goal. Looks a lot like the yoke, doesn't it? The yoke and the cross are both made of wood. They are both symbols of suffering. I truly believe that is the essence of coming to Jesus for rest. When you come and take the yoke it is a call to come and bear the cross—to come and die.

Mark 8:34-38 says, "*And when he had called the people unto him with his disciples also, he said unto them, Whosoever will come after me, let him deny himself, and take up his cross, and follow me. For whosoever will save his life shall lose it; but whosoever shall lose his life for my sake and the gospel's, the same shall save it. For what shall it profit a man, if he shall gain the whole world, and lose his own soul? Or what shall a man give in exchange for his soul? Whosoever therefore shall be ashamed of me and of my words in this adulterous and sinful generation; of him also shall the Son of man be ashamed, when he cometh in the glory of his Father with the holy angels.*"

There are a lot of people who want to follow Christ but don't want to take up their cross. We want rest, but we also set a place at the table for our selfish ambitions and desires. Selflessness is simply less of self and more of Jesus. More perfectly, selflessness is death to self and life to Jesus. Not the other way around.

I'm reminded of the story of the man who went to an older saint and asked, "What is it to be dead?" The saint told him to go visit Brother Thomas who had recently died, and to call him all the vile and contemptuous names he could think of, and to see what the dead man would reply. The man went down to the grave and cursed Brother Thomas in every way he could think. Then he stopped to listen for a reply—nothing.

So the preacher asked the man to go back down to the cemetery and flatter Brother Thomas and praise him in every possible way. He did. Still no reply. Upon his return the preacher said, "That is what it means to be dead. To not be moved by what is said against us or by praises that are given us." [22]

Dying to self is one of the hardest things you will ever do. You feel empty, broken, and desperate. A.W Tozer put it this way: "In every Christian's heart there is a cross and a throne, and the Christian is on the throne till he puts himself on the cross. If he refuses the cross he remains on the throne. Perhaps this is at the bottom of the backsliding and worldliness among gospel believers today. We want to be saved but we insist that Christ do all the dying. No cross for us, no dethronement, no dying. We remain king within the little kingdom of Mansoul and wear our tinsel crown with all the pride of a Caesar, but we doom ourselves to shadows and weakness and spiritual sterility." [23]

Think back in your mind to the Garden of Gethsemane. Jesus was pleading with His Father to *"let this cup pass from me,"* (Matthew 26:39). He knew the agony of the cross. He knew the pain that was ahead. He knew the rejection that awaited Him, and by the end of His supplication He bid, *"not my will, but thine, be done,"* (Luke 22:42). That is the process—putting our will aside for His.

George Muller wrote in his journal, "There was a day when I died, utterly died, died to George Muller, his opinions, preferences, tastes and will, died to the world, its approval or censure, died to the approval or blame even of my brethren and friends, and since then I have studied only to show myself approved unto God."

May I admit something to you? I am scared to death of death. Not of my physical death—that will be a glorious day when my faith becomes sight, and I see my Lord. I am afraid to die to Tyler because Tyler is whole-heartedly desperate to live. I want things my way and on my terms. I want to follow my plans and live the life I want to live.

We all have our reasons to "live," don't we? We all have excuses for not binding up our sinful desires and placing them on the altar. Do you identify with any of these?

It's too hard. The constant fight to stay right with God is exhausting. But Jesus will *"make a way of escape, that ye may be able to bear it,"* (I Corinthians 10:13).

"But he knoweth the way that I take: when he hath tried me, I shall come forth as gold," (Job 23:10).

It's too painful. Death brings pain. It is just a fact of life. Some people are afraid to step into the yoke because they are scared of experiencing more hurt. They want rest from their troubles but are not willing to leave their troubles with Jesus.

Philippians 3:7-8 says, *"But what things were gain to me, those I counted loss from Christ. Yea doubtless, and I count all things but loss for the excellency of the knowledge of Christ Jesus my Lord: for whom I suffered the loss of all things, and do count them but dung, that I may win Christ."*

It's too costly. We believe the lie that the yoke is too restricting. We panic over the thought of losing control if we are forever hitched with Jesus. Have you noticed that we panic over what we put value on? Like when we are in a hurry, and we just can't seem to find our wallet, we start to panic and brink on the edge of absolute insanity. Our blood pressure rises as our minds think about some homeless guy somewhere with our wallet running up the credit card.

Let's just be simple. We love our selves! We pamper, fix-up, and spend a great deal of money making sure we look the part of a Hollywood star prancing down the red carpet. This is why the yoke seems unattractive to us. We value ourselves greater than we value our Lord. Soul rest looks good on the shelf, but we are not willing to write the check to pay for it.

So what is it about self that must die? When we get in the yoke and step into Christ's classroom of meekness, what is it about us that dies?

Our Present Desires

Selflessness means death to your plans. Death to your dreams and aspirations. It is a burning of the calendar that steps into the unknown and wholly follows His lead. When you take the yoke upon you, you begin to learn that *"ye are not your own...for ye are bought with a price:"* (I Corinthians 6:19-20).

You know, I imagine it would be difficult to tell a blind man which way to walk, if he doesn't admit the fact that he is blind. I wonder if Christ feels that way with us sometimes.

We are blind without Him, destined for destruction, but Christ stoops down and heals our blinded eyes so that they may see His face. David reminds us, *"Show me thy O Lord; teach me thy paths.*

Lead me in thy truth, and teach me: for thou art the God of my salvation; on thee do I wait all the day," (Psalms 25:4-5).

Our Past Deeds

Sometimes restlessness comes in the form of a guilty conscience. We simply cannot get over the past failures that have brought darkness and pain into the picture. This is why we become bound by our own perfectionism; we are determined not to feel the pain of the past any longer.

It was a great day in my life when the Holy Spirit pricked my heart with this question: "Why are you content to hold onto what God has already let go of?" It struck me like a dart guided to the bulls-eye of my guilt. Why am I holding on?

Sometimes I hold on to my failures because it supplies a convenient cop-out. It negates me of future responsibility since I am convinced that I am a cripple. Other times I simply just can't let it go. But I do have help when it comes to being reminded of my "skeletons." The devil does everything he can to keep fresh in my mind the times that I abandoned my God for idols. Isn't it amazing? The one who tempts me to do evil, turns around and accuses me the moment I give in! That is his work. He is the tempter and *"accuser of our brethren,"* (Revelation 12:10).

But I've noticed something about being in Christ's yoke. You cannot look behind you. When you labor in the yoke with Christ, your past becomes just that—your past. What is plowed is plowed, and you begin to learn of His meekness and become dead to the power of the past.

I am often reminded of the words of C. S. Lewis: "Getting over a painful experience is much like crossing monkey bars. You have to let go at some point in order to move forward."

Other Peoples' Discussion

Meekness truly becomes meekness, when tried by the fires of other people's treatment of you. Think of our Lord. So gentle. So kind. So loving. And yet so mistreated. If you are reading these words, you have been mistreated in your lifetime. There is no way around it. But, with great hurt comes an opportunity of an even greater miracle.

Pastor Rick Finley often says, "Power belongs to the one who chooses to be submissive." There is great power in silence. Especially when we choose silence in moments of mistreatment and hurt. Our world today talks a lot about speaking out and raising your voice, but I'll remind you that Christ, in His moments of trial, did not answer a word. There is a time to preach truth and shout it from the rooftops, but there are other times when we must stop and be submissive.

Retaliation is a part of our nature, but so is restlessness. And every time we retaliate with a harsh comment on social media, roll our eyes at a brother in Christ, or respond critically to them that have the rule over us; we are setting the course for a very restless and miserable life.

The words of the hymn, "Not I, but Christ," incapsulate this truth so beautifully:

> *Not I but Christ be honored, loved, exalted*
> *Not I but Christ be seen be known be heard*
> *Not I but Christ in every look and action*
> *Not I but Christ in every thought and word*

If we want rest, these are things we must do daily just as Paul did: *"I protest by your rejoicing which I have in Christ Jesus our Lord, I die daily,"* (I Corinthians 15:31). We must die to our

86

present desires, our past deeds, and others discussion toward us. It is through this selflessness and through our suffering that we learn the lesson of the yoke.

CHAPTER EIGHT

The Promise of Rest

"...and ye shall find rest unto your souls."

I can't tell you exactly what was running through my head. All I know is that I was ready. Ready with bated breath and a quivering hand to pull the trigger. With eyes locked on the door, I secured my grip and waited for the henges to unlatch.

My wife, one-year-old daughter, and I had had a pretty good week. Well, as good as you can have in a new home, a new city, a new way of life. There is something so strange about uprooting years of habits and familiar scenery—something so final. Reality doesn't quite settle in at first as you almost trick yourself into thinking this is temporary. Once all the boxes are out of the moving truck and the furniture is in its designated spots, it seems almost outlandish that you are putting your belongings into someone else's home. But here we are.

Despite the challenges of a big move and the millions of questions left unanswered, we were excited to discover all that the Lord had in store for us in our new setting. Being on the pastoral staff was something I had dreamed about as little boy. God put it into my heart early on, and I was itching to serve Him in this new capacity under a faithful and godly mentor.

We were only a few weeks in when it happened.

I was sitting in "Daddy's chair" rocking my sweet Lilly to sleep. Things outside seemed a little unsettled; something strange was in the air. In fact, I had already done my manly nighttime security check to make sure all Robertsons were safe and sound. Earlier that evening, I had heard what sounded like voices outside our back window. So, I did what any protective husband or daddy would do; I grabbed the ole 9mm just in case of a neighborhood showdown. We had moved to a pretty, shall I say, needy community; and on one end of our street, there was nothing but trouble. I prepared accordingly.

Some time passed since I had heard the noises outside; and by this point, we were all starting to nod off from a long day. As I snuggled up to my little girl on our big comfy chair in the living room and my wife relaxed on the couch, I closed my eyes and started to drift away to sleepy land. Suddenly, I heard a loud "BOOM!" as the front door seemed to bow off its hinges. Someone was trying to get into our house with all of us in the living room and the lights on! Right away I knew this could not be a late-night Amazon delivery, so I jumped up as fast as I could.

I quickly grabbed my gun and darted to our bedroom. I threw Lilly on the bed, who had somehow managed to stay asleep during this entire episode, and I yelled to Kathryn,

"Call the police!"

As she fumbled through the dial on her phone, I pulled my gun out of the holster. I'm pretty sure my heart was in my throat at some point, but I would have to verify that with my doctor.

I took a defensive stance behind an adjacent doorway and pointed my 1911 toward the front door. It is amazing how many thoughts can go through your head in half a millisecond! I took a deep breath and braced for the next blow. I knew that all it would take was one more kick, and the intruder would be in my living room, leaving me with a life-or-death ultimatum. I wasn't going to stop and ask many questions or invite him over for tea first. The line had been crossed, and I was going to take the steps necessary to fulfill my role as the defender of my family. Through my fleeting breath, I started to pray:

"Lord, give me wisdom."

I waited for the night to pierce its way through our living room door and reveal the offender's identity. Even with my body screaming at me for more air, I held back the impulse and listened as intently as I could.

Nothing. No noise. No voices. Nothing.

I scurried to a nearby window to take a look outside for any radar on our suspect. I saw about five figures rustling in the shadows by their vehicles. Immediately my alert level peeked.

"When the cops get here, maybe they will scatter and go away," I thought.

Little did I know that the police wouldn't show up for the next hour as I paced the floor of the living room, checking every window and door.

To God be the glory, nothing tragic happened that night. All of us were safe and sound, and thankfully I did not have to make a life-altering decision.

I have thought about that night many times and am grateful for the Lord's goodness to us. Two lessons will forever be engraved on my mind: One, I'm glad I had a gun. Two, soul rest transcends difficult circumstances.

It was amazing. In those moments of uncertainty and anxiousness, there was a compelling notion in my soul that Jesus was right there with me, hushing every fear that tried to gain ground in my mind. It was truly a calm of the inner man that derived from an overwhelming belief that Jesus was in control. It was everything I had been learning in Matthew 11 chalked up in one single moment. I believed He would merit me rest, and I found it in Him.

The word *find* in Matthew 11:29 implies an obtainment or discovery. It's the result of drawing near to His person, the gift of accepting His product, the diploma of learning His process, and the hope of believing His promise. Soul rest is guaranteed to you: *"and ye shall find."* Jesus didn't make it up to trick you. He didn't devise a trap to lure you in so He could hurt you. He promises you soul rest. And trust me, He doesn't break His promises.

Que the probing question: Do you believe His promise?

Jesus' words in Matthew 11 are no good to you if you don't believe they are true. If you think that soul rest is a certain impossibility wrapped in adorned speech, then you will find it hard to maintain peace in difficult times. What sustained me that night of our "friendly visit" was not my physical strength or preparation, it was my faith in the promises of Christ. But lest you think I am presumptuous; I will be the first to admit it was nothing of my doing. Christ had done all of the work and led me to receive it. The promise of soul rest was true, whether I acknowledged it or not. The difference was that the Word had been applied and manifested itself even in the restlessness around me.

Many people never find rest for their souls because they do not believe in His promise that they *"will find"* if only they will *"come."* But it is belief in this promise and unwavering faith in His character that triumphs over difficulty. Faith anchors the heart through troubled waters and keeps you safe at His side.

First Peter 1:8 reminds us, *"Whom having not seen, ye love; in whom, though now ye see him not, yet believing, ye rejoice with joy unspeakable and full of glory:"* There is rejoicing and joy unspeakable for the Christian who chooses to believe what he cannot see. Faith is the expectancy of the mountain in the midst of a dark valley. It is reaching out to the Hand of promise and truth through the billowing clouds of doubt and confusion. It is a denial of tangible elements for the expectancy of eternal ones.

Hebrews 11:1 and 6 explain it for us: *"Now faith is the substance of things hoped for, the evidence of things not seen . . . But without faith it is impossible to please him: for he that cometh to God must believe that he is, and that he is a rewarder of them that diligently seek him."*

This is the faith we are to walk in: *"(For we walk by faith, not by sight:)"* (II Corinthians 5:7).

When we doubt Jesus' words, we have stepped off the beaten path of safety and security, causing us to become oblivious to our plight. Inevitable destruction. Remember Chapter 4?

We saw what the dangers of pleasure do to the believer and how they lead to a world of distraction and misplaced dependency on the god of ease. Trying to escape the restlessness inside is like setting a glass bottle in the sea in hopes that the drifting of the tide will bring it to the shore. It is subject to the toil of the winds and waves of life. This is the result of unbelief in the words of God. It is a failure to exercise living faith, and that can only lead to compromise. Mark it down. Doubting leads to drifting. And when we turn our eyes to gaze on the path that we have chosen, we find a staunch contradiction to the life Jesus desires for us. How did we get here? Because we never believed Him.

I am confident in Charles Spurgeon's description of the believer that chooses to live in doubt and unbelief: "It is not the general habit of unbelief among God's people to give a flat contradiction to his promises: we are hardly honest enough to our own thoughts to express them with deliberate plainness of speech: even unbelief loves to wear some cobweb covering or other, that its naked deformity may not appear. Our reverence for the Lord will not permit us distinctly to give him the lie; but it comes to much the same thing, for in our heart of hearts we deny the truthfulness of his word." [24]

So again, you must answer: Do you believe His promise of rest? Can you fall on Jesus and know He will be there to catch you? Can you stop long enough for Jesus to heal your blinded eyes? Can you move in obedience to the truth that He speaks to you? Will you believe His promise of rest?

To answer this, we must, for last time, let the Word of our Lord cut deeply into our hearts. We must face our unbelief so that we may glory in His promise of soul rest! In this last chapter of our journey, we will take a look at three familiar stories found in the Gospel of Mark. Chapters 4-6 deal directly with the power of living faith, the danger of doubt, and the liberation of Christ's soul rest.

Believe Despite the Danger (Mark 4)

I love watching storms. I guess you can call me a little bit of a thrill seeker if you'd like. Sitting down under a porch is my preferred position for watching the rain dance through a velvet lining of mountainous clouds, broken by the glow of electric impulses. There is something so enriching about it all that awakens my senses and reminds me how small I am in this big world we live in. Storms have a way of reminding us who we are and Who our Creator is. Just ask the disciples.

When you turn the pages of your Bible to Mark chapter 4, you are met with many parables that pack a punch for faith and fruitfulness. Jesus begins on the sea side, teaching His followers the parable of the sower and the importance of their heart conditions to His words. He labors His point further as His disciples are confused about the symbolism of His message. It is all a strategic plan of the Master as He prepares His pupils to meet one of their greatest challenges. This storm would not be one for the casual observer or thrill seeker; it was a matter of life and death.

"And the same day, when the even was come, he saith unto them, Let us pass over unto the other side. And when they had sent away the multitude, they took him even as he was in the ship. And there were also with him other little ships. And there arose a great storm of wind, and the waves beat into the ship, so that it was now full. And he was in the hinder part of the ship, asleep on a pillow: and they awake him, and say unto him, Master, carest thou not that we perish? And he arose, and rebuked the wind, and said unto the sea, Peace, be still. And the wind ceased, and there was a great calm. And he said unto them, Why are ye so fearful? how is it that ye have no faith? And they feared exceedingly, and said one to another, What manner of man is this, that even the wind and the sea obey him?" (Mark 4:35-41).

There is something so compelling about Jesus' wonderful words in these verses: *"Peace be still."* Etched into the fabric of our soul is a longing for Jesus to speak this truth to our restless hearts. We are so shaken and moved by the winds and waves of this world and our hearts cry out as the Psalmist: *"By terrible things in righteousness wilt thou answer us, O God of our salvation; who art the confidence of all the ends of the earth, and of them that are afar off upon the sea: Which by his strength setteth fast the mountains; being girded with power: Which stilleth the noise of the seas, the noise of their waves, and the tumult of the people,"* (Psalm 65:5-7).

Stillness removes the trembling fear and ushers in Christ's promise of peace. But remember, faith in His promise is what we are after, not just a mere awareness that His promise exists.

Notice the compelling truths of the story that connect stillness with lingering faith.

They were given direction. What did Jesus say to His followers? *"Let us pass over onto the other side."* This was not a whimsical alternative, or a plan "B"; this was a pre-charted course that the Master knew very well. Christ knew the storm would meet them in the midst, but His direction did not change.

This is the Lord's direction for us. It is not around the storm. It is not over the storm. It is *through* the storm that Christ can create in us *"the righteousness of God revealed from faith to faith,"* (Romans 1:17).

Oftentimes our faith hits a stumbling block because we do not trust His direction. We are so restless, hustling through life trying to chart our own course or find a pleasure that will. Living by faith in the promises of Christ lies at the intersection of your will and Christ's way. You must choose one or the other. You must believe that His direction is best, even if there are dark clouds in the distance.

They were hindered by danger. It was not uncommon for storms to swiftly develop over the Sea of Galilee. It was almost expected anytime a fisherman lifted the anchor and set out the nets for a day's work. So what was the big deal? I mean, weren't several of the disciples skilled fishermen and used to the storms of the sea? Did they adequately prepare for the storm? Did it catch them off guard? Perhaps. But whatever our suppositions, we can adamantly conclude that this storm made a ship full of tough fishermen fearfully declare their own death.

It is my firm conviction that the prospect of danger is one of the greatest hindrances of abandoned surrender to Christ. His way is not always easy. It does not always seem safe. Remember my gunslinging story? That wasn't safe. In fact, it was terrifying! But God allowed it to happen and taught me many things through it. Danger keeps us in the land of uncertainty, and uncertainty demands that we live by faith in His promises.

They were wrestling with doubt. *"Why are ye so fearful? how is it that ye have no faith?"* Herein we find the great connection we have visited many times in this book. The battle between fear and faith. What was their fear? It was the storm, yes, but it was also the fact that Jesus was quiet in the midst of their trial. He was asleep! Silent. Absent. "Not aware" of their struggle.

Isn't this the essence of not finding rest for our souls? We simply don't believe that He cares. But "never doubt in the dark what God has revealed to you in the light" (Unknown).

They were amazed at the declaration. Christ stood boldly on the bough of the ship and rebuked the wind and commanded the sea to be still. Think about the disciples' reactions. *"What manner of man is this that even the wind and sea obey him?"* I think often times we see our storm to be bigger than our God. We forget the transformative power of His words and the authority that He has over all of our circumstances. *"He maketh the storm a calm, so that the waves thereof are still"* (Psalm 107:29).

Living faith in the promises of Jesus will undeniably bring stillness into your life. *"Be still, and know that I am God: I will be exalted among the heathen, I will be exalted in the earth,"* (Psalm 46:10).

Do you believe His promise despite the danger?

Believe Despite the Delay (Mark 5)

Notice these encouraging words at the very onset of Chapter 5: *"and they came over onto the other side of the sea."* Just as Jesus had promised, they arrived at their destination safe and sound.

But I want to turn your attention briefly to a man by the name of Jairus in Mark chapter 5. He was a husband. A father. A religious official. And, no doubt, a good man. But he needed Jesus because his precious little girl was deathly ill. And so, Jairus *"besought him greatly, saying, My little daughter lieth at the point of death: I pray thee, come and lay thy hands on her, that she may be healed; and she shall live,"* (vs. 23). Can you imagine the pain and urgency in his voice? I have two precious daughters, and I can't fathom the prospect of standing in his shoes.

Jesus, in His compassion, *"went with him."*

However, the prospect of a new miracle ushered in an enormous crowd trying to follow Jesus, insomuch that the crowd pressed against Him. Jairus was not the only one that needed Jesus' attention that day. Lost amidst the crowd, there was a woman who had had an issue of blood some twelve years. She had tried everything to cure her disease, but even the greatest physicians could do nothing for her. She eventually fought her way into close proximity with Christ. In desperation, she reached for the hem of His garment. *"And Jesus, immediately knowing in himself that virtue had gone out of him, turned him about in the press, and said, Who touched my clothes? And his disciples said unto him, Thou seest the multitude thronging thee, and sayest thou, Who touched me?"* (vv. 30-31).

In essence they were saying, "What do you mean 'Who touched you?' There are all these people around you!" Many scholars believe that the road that Jesus was walking on at this time was very narrow, and what He felt could have easily been a pinch in a small crowd. Jesus knew. This is why He stopped and faced the woman with compassion.

But wait! Jairus. His daughter was dying. He still had an unmet need and time was of the essence. Can you imagine what he must have thought? "Jesus, we have to hurry! We do not have time for this! My daughter needs you!"

And yet Jesus stopped and took the time to heal a woman, saying to her: *"Daughter, thy faith hath made thee whole; go in peace, and be whole of thy plague,"* (vs. 34).

While Jesus was speaking, there came one of Jairus's servants with despairing news: *"Thy daughter is dead: why troublest thou the Master any further?"* (vs. 35). But Jesus hearing this, quickly rebuked the possibility of fear and turned to Jairus and spoke a profound truth: *"Be not afraid, only believe,"* (vs. 36).

With power in His voice, the command came to the damsel: *"Talithacumi; which is, being interpreted, Damsel, I say unto thee, arise. And straightway the damsel arose, and walked...and they were astonished with a great astonishment,"* (vv. 41-42).

God can see the end before the beginning. His plan did not seem to fit in Jairus's timeline, but God proved Himself to be a keeper of His promises, despite the delay.

Delays are not fun. They are inconvenient, unsettling, and questionable seasons of life. But when they are divine in nature, a delay may be just what is necessary for God to do a thorough work in you. It will not be on your schedule, and you will not always be prepared for it; but know with certainty that God will come through with His promises. My pastor advises us to "Never mistake God's delays as denial."

Do you believe His promise despite the delays?

Believe Despite the Deception (Mark 6)

After a quick turn-around of events, the disciples were right back in the thick of it. I wonder if their weary legs were getting feeble trying to keep up with Jesus. It seems there was opposition around every corner, industrializing their questions and trying their patience. But the sad reality of their seemingly directionless journey was characterized by the detour of doubt. Jesus and His followers arrived in a city; and as Scripture records on many accounts, He could do no mighty work because of their (the people's) unbelief.

We visit this again in Mark chapter 6, insomuch that Christ *"marveled because of their unbelief,"* (vs. 6). But I want to direct you to the last part of the chapter where we find another scary encounter with a contrary wind. This time things were a little different as Jesus instructed them to continue to the other side without Him. Jesus separated Himself *"into a mountain to pray"* (vs. 46) and watched as the disciples toiled through the darkness of the night, battling the blows of the wind and waves. After watching them struggle, Jesus miraculously set His course on the water's surface, paving a path through the sea. But it's the next phrase that begs a question for me: *"and would have passed by them,"* (vs. 48).

And would have passed by? Really? You mean He would have gone right past them without lending a hand? Why would Jesus do this? I believe it was for the same reason Jesus had to pass by many villages and towns: because of their unbelief. Jesus wanted to know if His disciples could recognize Him in the midst of their toil, and further, if they would call out to Him. Notice their reaction: *"But when they saw him walking upon the sea, they supposed it had been a spirit, and cried out: For they all saw him, and were troubled,"* (vv. 49-50a). But cue the powerful words of Christ: *"Be of good cheer; it is I; be not afraid,"* (Matthew 14:27).

Notice what the winds didn't do this time. They did not go away. Matthew's account of this story provides a little more drama. *"And Peter answered him and said, Lord, if it be thou, bid me come unto thee on the water. And he said, Come,"* (Matthew 14:28-29).

I believe we have come full circle. Jesus' cry to us at the beginning is the same now in the midst of a restless world. He says to Peter, *"Come. And when Peter was come down out of the ship, he walked on the water, to go to Jesus. But when he saw the wind boisterous, he was afraid; and beginning to sink, he cried, saying, Lord, save me. And immediately Jesus stretched forth his hand, and caught him, and said unto him, O thou of little faith, wherefore didst thou doubt?"* (Matthew 14:30-31).

This is the ultimatum that stands between us and rest for our souls. We can hear Him call, even take a step closer, and still doubt His promise to us. The winds of doubt are deceptive and delusional. They keep our eyes locked on uncertainty and pain. They claim that Jesus is just a figment of our imagination, just a spirit set out to cause fear. They stroke the enhancement of our pride and turn our eyes back to the ship of reason. They grip at our hearts and pull us beneath the billows of despair. They slay our children and blind them to whimsical fancies of the world. They do not welcome faith. They do not usher in peace. Our doubts rebel against the very nature of Christ. They curse and mock Him to scorn. They will insist that rest will never come.

Do you believe His promise despite the deception?

***

Facing our unbelief is not simple for any of us. It is easy to doubt in the middle of danger, delay, or deception. The nation of Israel understood what it was to face that battle and lose: *"Thus saith the LORD, Stand ye in the ways, and see, and ask for the old paths, where is the good way, and walk therein, and ye shall find rest for your souls. But they said, We will not walk therein. Also I set watchmen over you, saying, Hearken to the sound of the trumpet. But they said, We will not hearken,"* (Jeremiah 6:16-17).

God was saying to His people that there was a way of rest for them. It was completely different than the world's way. It was not through prosperity. It was not in their own productivity. It could not be found in the legislation of perfectionism. And it would not be through fleshly pleasure. God's rest would be gifted through the promises of Christ and His eternal Word. *"But they said, We will not hearken."* They missed it. Their rest was there. They just missed it.

Do not miss what Jesus is saying to you. Enter into His presence on your knees and hear His promise: *"Come unto me, all ye that labour and are heavy laden, and I will give you rest. Take my yoke upon you, and learn of me; for I am meek and lowly in heart: and ye shall find rest unto your souls. For my yoke is easy, and my burden is light,"* (Matthew 11:28-30).

Do you believe Him?

Works Cited

1 McCallen, Jon. "The Self-Storage Self," *New York Times*, September 2, 2009.

2 Hill, Catey. "The Dark Reasons So Many Rich People Are Miserable Human Beings," *Market Watch*, February 22, 2018, https://www.google.com/amp/s/www.marketwatch.com/amp/story/the-dark-reasons-so-many-rich-people-are-miserable-human-beings-2018-02-22

3 Hou, Staphany. "Monkeys More Selfish Than Once Thought," *Yale Daily News*, November 18, 2014, https://yaledailynews.com/blog/2014/11/18/monkeys-more-selfish-than-once-thought/

4 Polk, Sam. "For the Love of Money," *New York Times*, January 18, 2014, http://www.nytimes.com/2014/01/19/opinion/sunday/for-the-love-of-money.html

5 Ortberg, John. *The Life You've Always Wanted.* Grand Rapids, MI: Zondervan, 2009.

6 Comer, John Mark. *The Ruthless Elimination of Hurry.* Colorado Springs, CO: Waterbrook, 2019.

7 Zimbardo, Philip; Sword, Richard; & Sword, Rosemary. *The Time Cure, Overcoming PTSD with the New Psychology of TIme Perspective Therapy.* Hoboken, NJ: Jossey-Bass, 2012.

8 Zigarelli, Michael. "Distracted from God: A Five-Year, Worldwide Study," *Christianity 9 to 5,* 2012, www.christianity9to5.org/distracted-from-god

9 Comer, 2019.

10 P, Kim. "Study: Average Cost of a Vacation," *Credit Donkey,* July 14, 2022, https://www.creditdonkey.com/average-cost-vacation.html

11 Greig, Jonathan. "Average Consumer Spending," *ZDNet*, September 21, 2021, https://www.zdnet.com/article/average-consumer-spending-273-per-month-on-subscription-services-report/

12 Clement, J. "Consumer Spending on Video Game Content in the U.S.," *Statista*, April 29, 2022, https://www.statista.com/chart/9838/consumer-spending-on-video-games/

[13] Comer, 2019.

[14] "Television Watching Statistics," *Statistic Brain Research Institute,* May 23, 2017, https://www.statisticbrain.com/television-watching-statistics/

[15] Wheelwright, Trevor. "2022 Cell Phone Usage Statistics: How Obsessed Are We?" *Reviews.org,* January 24, 2022, https://www.reviews.org/mobile/cell-phone-addiction

[16] Bonhoeffer, Dietrich. *Creation and Fall Temptation: Two Biblical Studies.* Manhattan, NY: Simon and Schuster, 1959.

[17] Carson, D. A. *For the Love of God, Vol. 2.* Wheaton, IL: Crossway, 2006.

[18] Zacharias, Ravi. "The Problem of Pleasure," *YouTube*, October 8, 2010, http://m.youtube.com/watch?v=wLvOCXDho0

[19] Spurgeon, Charles Haddon. "The Immutability of Christ," *The Spurgeon Center,* January 3, 1858, http://www.spurgeon.org/resource-library/sermons/the-immutability-of-christ/

[20] Spurgeon, Charles Haddon. "A Sense of Pardoned Sin," *The Spurgeon Center*, May 20, 1860, http://www.spurgeon.org/resource-library/sermons/a-sense-of-pardoned-sin/

[21] Strongs Concordance. "Galatians 5:23," *Blue Letter Bible,* August 18, 2022, https://www.blueletterbible.org/lang/lexicon/lexicon.cfm?Strongs=G4239&ss=

[22] Barbour, B. McCall. *When Did You Die.* Powell, TN: Faith for the Family.

[23] Tozer, A. W. *The Radical Cross: Living the Passion of Christ.* Camp Hill, PA: Wing Spread Publishers.

[24] Spurgeon, Charles Haddon. (1883). *Metropolitan Tabernacle Pulpit, Vol. 29.*

About the Author

Tyler Robertson is an assistant pastor, high school teacher, and writer. He has a huge passion for preaching God's Word, and he strives to love and serve others. He and his wife, Kathryn, have three beautiful children: Lilly, Annabelle, and Trevor. He enjoys spending time with his family and serving the Lord alongside a wonderful church family.

Tyler is also the host of the Navigator's Podcast. You can tune in wherever you listen to podcasts. You may also find other great resources and writings at tylerarobertson.com.

Connect with Tyler here:

Blog: tylerarobertson.com

Twitter: twitter.com/@T_Robertson333

Facebook: facebook.com/TylerARobertson3

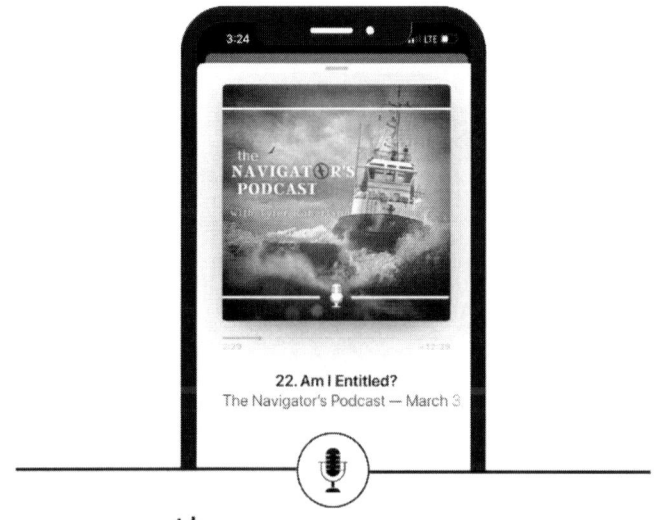

the
NAVIGAT⊕R'S
PODCAST

Join us on the Navigator's Podcast as we equip men and women to steer the course of biblical Christianity in our culture today. Each week we discuss faith, family, and the cultural trends that are sure to impact the local church.

tylerarobertson.com/listen